CW00349014

AT THE MARGINS

Despite the tremendous progress in the development of scientific knowledge, the understanding of the causes of poverty and inequality, and the role of politics and governance in addressing modern challenges, issues such as social inclusion, poverty, marginalization and despair continue to be a reality across the world – and most often impact Indigenous Peoples. *At the Margins of Globalization* explores how Indigenous Peoples are affected by globalization, and the culture of individual choice without responsibility that it promotes, while addressing what can be done about it. Though international trade and investment agreements are unlikely to go away, the inclusion of Indigenous rights provisions has made a positive difference. This book explains how these provisions operate and how to build from their limited success.

SERGIO PUIG is Professor of Law and Director of the International Trade and Business Law Program at the University of Arizona. He specializes in free trade agreements, international investment law and dispute settlement, with a particular focus on the NAFTA (now USMCA), as well as economic rights of Indigenous Peoples. Before entering academia, he practiced international law and arbitration, and worked as a diplomat at the World Bank Group.

GLOBALIZATION AND HUMAN RIGHTS

The series provides unique and multi-disciplinary perspectives on the interface of the global economy and human rights. It offers space for exploring the challenges of globalization, the role of human rights in framing and shaping regulation and politics and, more critically, whether human rights are a mere product or legitimation of globalization.

Series Editors

Malcolm Langford

César Rodríguez-Garavito

Forthcoming Books in the Series

Jeremy Perelman, *The Rights-ification of Development: Global Poverty, Human Rights, and Globalization in the Post-Washington Consensus*

At the Margins of Globalization

INDIGENOUS PEOPLES AND
INTERNATIONAL ECONOMIC LAW

SERGIO PUIG

University of Arizona

CAMBRIDGE
UNIVERSITY PRESS

CAMBRIDGE
UNIVERSITY PRESS

University Printing House, Cambridge CB2 8BS, United Kingdom

One Liberty Plaza, 20th Floor, New York, NY 10006, USA

477 Williamstown Road, Port Melbourne, VIC 3207, Australia

314-321, 3rd Floor, Plot 3, Splendor Forum, Jasola District Centre, New Delhi - 110025, India

103 Penang Road, #05-06/07, Visioncrest Commercial, Singapore 238467

Cambridge University Press is part of the University of Cambridge.

It furthers the University's mission by disseminating knowledge in the pursuit of education, learning and research at the highest international levels of excellence.

www.cambridge.org
Information on this title: www.cambridge.org/9781108740197
DOI: 10.1017/9781108596503

First published 2021
First paperback edition 2022

A catalogue record for this publication is available from the British Library

ISBN 978-1-108-49764-0 Hardback
ISBN 978-1-108-74019-7 Paperback

Cambridge University Press has no responsibility for the persistence or accuracy of URLs for external or third-party internet websites referred to in this publication, and does not guarantee that any content on such websites is, or will remain, accurate or appropriate.

To Sabrina Puig Robles
To Negar, Diego and Daria

Contents

Tables

Preface and Acknowledgments

Scholarship on the links between business and human rights is widespread. However, the specific ways in which globalization accommodates the economically marginalized and those who are likely most vulnerable to its negative effects has received scant attention. The increasingly obvious manifestations of discontent over the effects of globalization – from Brexit to the election of President Trump – combined with the evidence that confirms the very uneven distribution of its benefits, indicate that this is an important scholarly gap.

This book explores the extent to which the main fields of international law that are tasked with promoting economic interdependence – international finance, investment, trade and intellectual property – address the rights and interests of Indigenous peoples, an expressly protected category of marginalized and/or vulnerable people under international law. Relying on recent legal practice and eight case studies, the book compares these fields and explains the different ways Indigenous peoples' interests are accommodated by international economic law. More broadly, the intersection between international economic law and indigenous rights provides important lessons for current demands to address the negative effects of globalization.

The book is the result of the author's experiences and perspectives working with different institutions including the World Bank Group as well as with the Committee for Mexico's Legal and Constitutional Reform Regarding Indigenous and Afromexican Peoples' Rights. I would like to thank S. James Anaya, Derek Bambauer, Tomer Broude, James Cavallaro, Anupam Chander, Andrew Coan, Seth Davis, David A. Gantz, Negar Katirai, Malcolm Langford, Cesar Rodriguez-Garavito, Lise Johnson, Jason Kreag, Robert A. Hershey, Moshe Hirsch, James Hopkins, Toni Massaro, David Marcus, Lauge Poulsen, Christopher T. Robertson, Rebecca Tsosie, Gregory Shaffer, Melissa L. Tatum, Steven R. Ratner, Adelfo Regino, Rebecca Tsosie, Robert

Williams, Mark Wu and the participants of workshops at the University of California, Irvine, University of Arizona, University of Colorado, University College London and the Hebrew University, for their helpful criticisms, advice, inspiration and/or suggestions for the book. Alancay Morales, Andrew J. Shepherd, Maxmilien Bradley and Benedict M. Nchalla, provided excellent research and editorial assistance. The book was made possible in part thanks to grants from the Lannan Foundation and the Arizona Summer Research Grant.

Cover image: Guarijio (Makurawe) Dancers in San Bernado, Álamos, Sonora, Mexico by Marsel Paulina Bermúdez Gaona, INPI.

Introduction

The images are harsh, ubiquitous and recurrent. As this book goes to print, the Navajo Nation in the United States continues to grapple with what is America's worst Covid-19 outbreak. In 2019 Jair Bolsonaro, Brazil's authoritarian, racist leader praised the genocide of Indigenous people and moved to revoke the protected status of indigenous lands. In the Philippines, 164 environmental activists – most of them indigenous – were murdered at the hands of Duterte's government in 2018 for defending their homes, lands and natural resources from exploitation. In 2017 a homeless girl from the indigenous Mbya Guarani was captured drinking unclean water from a puddle to relieve her thirst in the midday sun as the temperature topped 100°F (38 °C) degrees in Argentina. In 2016 police with water cannons violently cleared, in 28 °F (−2 °C) weather, activists protesting to stop the development of a pipeline that threatens the Standing Rock Indian Reservation's water supply. Sadly, one can go on and on with heartbreaking vignettes of different forms of indignity, injustice, discrimination and violence suffered by Indigenous peoples all across the world.

Despite the tremendous progress in the development of scientific knowledge, in the understanding of the structural causes of poverty and inequality and in the role of politics and governance in addressing modern challenges, social inclusion, poverty, marginalization and despair is a reality across the world – from wealthy America to middle-income Argentina to the less wealthy Philippines. And very often this reality has an indigenous face.

This reality is particularly painful for many who like me, enjoy visiting Mexico, the beautifully complex country where I grew up. Despite some progress and the tremendous wealth of many who are economically privileged, including the once richest man on Earth (Carlos Slim), marginalization in Mexico tends to follow skin color; the imperfect, accented Spanish that results from speaking another language; a huipil (a traditional

1

indigenous dress) the smell of copal; the wearing of sandals. For years, I was aware of this (and of my privilege as a white man), but in assisting Professor James Anaya's work on the Duty to Consult and with the Committee for the Legal and Constitutional Reform regarding Indigenous and Afromexican Peoples' Rights, I realized that many of Mexico's current problems are rooted in the unspoken structural racism against Indigenous peoples. I am not alone in this sentiment. It is now well accepted by the main UN agencies, scholars and policymakers that tackling "gross inequalities" within and between countries is necessary for addressing the major issues impacting our global community, including conflict, climate justice and mass "irregular" migrations.

This book is an attempt to contribute to the search for solutions to inequality and marginalization. It does so first by dissecting how the frameworks and institutions that encourage economic interdependence between countries tend to aggravate problems – such as poverty, political disfranchisement and social exclusion – already faced by indigenous communities. Second, the book describes the goals and functioning of the protections included in these arrangements to illuminate some avenues for reform based on the (limited) successful experiences of indigenous advocates in navigating the complex web of institutions for global economic governance. In providing these plausible but modest solutions, I am well aware that resolving globalization's negative effects on marginalized groups will not result from simple administrative or technical solutions. The current dysfunction of liberal capitalistic societies, many embedded in a culture of unconstrained freedom, individual choice and consumption with limited responsibility toward both our planet and our shared futures, calls for a more active and radical reimagining of the state and its relationship with production, distribution and consumption. Moreover, as an international economic law professor specializing in the notoriously controversial field of international investment law, I am keenly aware of the failures of international law. Too often, international law has been used to dismiss Indigenous peoples with arrogant and ignorant opinions and statements, including that "[s]ome tribes are so low in the scale of social organization that their usages and conceptions of rights and duties are not to be reconciled with the institutions or legal ideas of civilized society."[1]

That being said, I also believe that understanding the ways in which international economic law can exacerbate marginalization is necessary. At the same time, the notion that "For our nations to live, capitalism must die" – a popular

---

[1]   In re Southern Rhodesia (60) (1919) AC 211, pp. 233–234, per Lord Sumner, quoted in Mabo decision, p. 39. See *Race and Empire in the Mabo Decision. Symposium Issue of Social Identities*, Autumn 1997, at SSRN: https://ssrn.com/abstract=1002209.

refrain for many indigenous activists opposed to international investment and trade – is rather vague, improbable in the short term and impossible to cross-examine with more objective analysis. Trade and investment agreements are unlikely to go away, and the inclusion of human rights provisions have made a positive difference in the lives of some of the people they are intended – on paper, at least – to protect. We can build from this success.

Without discounting the fact that the shift of the required magnitude to address the issue of marginalization and the challenges faced by globalization can only be procured and legitimized through politics; through the contest of values, morals, beliefs and feelings; and through the transformation of domestic rules and regulations, this book relates to three different strands of literature of international law.

On the one hand, there is a rich debate regarding the role of human rights law as a source to constrain multinational businesses. This literature has been advanced by business and human rights, corporate social responsibility as well as social justice and international law scholars. Here, the book adds two interesting dimensions to such literature: First, it reveals how human rights advocacy can effectively be expanded using tools from outside the contours of what is traditionally defined as international human rights law and its institutions. It also provides an additional layer of analysis by incorporating Indigenous peoples' rights and policy perspectives as an example of marginalized populations. Here the contribution of the book is to describe and contrast, both in theory and in action, the effectiveness of international trade, investment, finance and intellectual property laws in the accommodation of Indigenous peoples' rights and interests. The analysis renders some evidence that the regimes of economic interdependence provide a growing set of possibilities for those who seek to advance indigenous rights and interests using international economic law. In addition to reinforcing economic freedoms for business actors, these regimes could be used to: (1) to expose the negative effects of the operations of multinational corporations on indigenous communities; (2) to strengthen the capacity of states and international organizations to protect indigenous rights; (3) to condition access to economic benefits on the support of indigenous interests; and (4) to provide policy incentives that promote indigenous products and the practices associated with their production.

On the other hand, a related line of literature, exemplified by S. James Anaya's classic study *Indigenous Peoples in International Law* (Oxford University Press) and Patrick Macklem's *The Sovereignty of Human Rights* (Cambridge University Press) emphasize the emancipatory capacity of human rights law in providing tools to safeguard against (but also advocate within) the state. This book draws from these rich descriptions and analyses to argue for the expanded use of human rights of Indigenous peoples within international economic arrangements as a mitigating force against the imbalance of power created by these international business frameworks. As framed, the book explains how international economic law fails to promote liberal values by creating a potentially devastating political economy when international law is advanced, unconstrained, as a tool to facilitate a "neutral" market order system. This dynamic exacerbates vast disparities in capabilities and material resources in both political and economic domains. Not only does the book provide a rich set of potential innovations to limit such impacts on Indigenous peoples (and potentially other marginalized and/or vulnerable populations), but links this argument to more theoretical approaches regarding the role of law (in this case, international law) in modern capitalistic societies.

Finally, the apparently endemic failure of globalization to address market-driven inequalities in income, wealth or access to goods and services has reinvigorated a debate over the effectiveness of international law. In particular, calls to limit the role of international law are growing among influential policymakers. Many have advocated "economic nationalism" and the termination of international economic agreements. This book is a response in part to the ways in which the failures of globalization have been framed, ignoring the years of calls for social inclusion and a fairer playing field. Here the book suggests that there is a place for vulnerable and marginalized groups, Indigenous peoples among them, within international economic law, and serves as a qualified defense of international law. It is also a call to reorient the debate about the future of globalization and to move beyond the false claims that the excesses of globalization are imposed by exogenous forces (e.g., immigrants and refugees, Muslims, China) and felt mostly by semi-skilled industrial workers. An international economic law that focuses on the vulnerable and marginalized can provide a limited yet important pathway for improving the unequal distribution of the benefits of globalization and for moving beyond the standard academic reply that redistribution should be a purely domestic policy response.

In addition to this introduction and a brief conclusion, the book is divided into seven chapters. The chapters are organized in three parts as I briefly summarize now.

Setting the Stage: The Negative Faces of Globalization

For centuries, indigenous groups have faced economic, physical and cultural subjugation. This does not seem to be ending anytime soon. Even if Indigenous peoples are not being intentionally deprived of land and wealth, they are being deprived of opportunity. In most countries, Indigenous peoples are worse off in relative terms than others who have benefited from a period of rapid growth and development. While this trend has been closely monitored by human rights advocates, it has been registered as white noise in the current debates over globalization's damaging effects.

As discussed in Chapter 1, to a large extent, the perspectives critical of globalization in international economic law have focused on the relative effects of globalization on the animation of different political causes. As I explain by reference to the work of scholars on globalization, there are multiple frames with which to see its problematic effects (as well as its real or perceived benefits). This book is concerned mainly with one particular frame; that of the groups subjugated and marginalized by the process of globalization. As I argue, these are groups truly left behind by the current form of economic interconnection whose voices have been only slightly and recently taken into account in this current wave of contestation. Conversely, it is precisely this perspective that might provide a fundamental lens for organizing transformative action. To contextualize the discussion, it is important to situate the perspective on globalization of these groups in opposition to other "narratives" driving debates about who wins and loses in modern times. Without a holistic approach to the different perspectives on the discontents of globalization, particularly given that all of the narratives reveal problematic aspects, it would be inadequate and misleading to address the issue of globalization and the marginalized without this context as a reference.

Chapter 2 provides a conceptual framework to understand the negative effects of globalization on vulnerable and marginalized groups. I term this framework "the cycle of susceptibility and exclusion." This framework illuminates the particular susceptibility of Indigenous peoples to the negative consequences of global economic interdependence and provides a point of reference to evaluate the effectiveness of existing and potential legal responses to that susceptibility. In short, the framework explains how international economic agreements often exacerbate vast disparities in capabilities and material resources in both political and economic domains. Politically, disenfranchisement results from the lack of direct participation of Indigenous peoples in the law production processes (treaty and adjudicatory lawmaking) and the indirect shift in governance priorities that results from enacting and enforcing treaty provisions (and resulting practices and interpretations). Economically, the focus on nondiscrimination among economic actors results in *de facto* discrimination against Indigenous peoples and a consequent rise in inequality.

International Indigenous Economic Law: An Emerging Field

Chapter 3 describes how the four main fields accommodate the rights and interests of Indigenous peoples. The question of who is indigenous is a complex question that I do not try to answer, in part because it also has been extensively debated. Instead, I adopt the definition that requires an "experience of subjugation, marginalization, dispossession, exclusion or discrimination." These elements are rooted in economic, social and political considerations, and have justified the development of rights owed to Indigenous peoples as a "class" – a group of people with common characteristics whose interests are legally protected. I also accept that there is no one single indigenous experience. Quite to the contrary, the experiences of Indigenous peoples are varied, and groups are occasionally rich and empowered. Yet, for most indigenous groups the likely result of instruments of globalization that enable unconstrained interdependence is an increase in relative inequality.

In summary, what this analysis reveals is that provisions exist within international economic arrangements for the protection of Indigenous peoples, but they are often under-enforced, weak or hamstrung by other forces. Protections tend to be stronger in IP, which creates *sui generis* rights, and finance, which relies on safeguards incorporated in loan agreements. Protections in international trade and investment tend to be weaker. These agreements regulate the relationship between distinct legal obligations through reservations, carve outs or exceptions. In all these regimes, the application of secondary rules of international law, like the rules of treaty interpretation are generally not excluded by treaties. Hence, these secondary rules might result in the elevation of legal protections enshrined in other sources of legal authority. Nevertheless, this analysis suggests that the regimes of economic interdependence provide a growing set of possibilities for those who seek to advance indigenous rights and interests using international economic law.

Chapter 4 describes eight case studies to explore the effectiveness of the four explored fields in the accommodation of Indigenous peoples. The cases involve indigenous communities in Africa and the Americas and show how indigenous interests have used different arrangements to resist the cycle of susceptibility and exclusion or to take advantage of economic liberalization when possible. Some of the cases incorporate my own experiences and perspectives working with different institutions between 2014 and 2019, thanks to Professor S. James Anaya, former United Nations Special Rapporteur on the Rights of Indigenous Peoples, and a (former) colleague at the University of Arizona, and during my visit at University of Colorado (where Professor Anaya sat as Dean of the Law School).

The analysis shows that while imperfect, international economic law could perform the function of *shield* for indigenous rights. As I explain, states have an undeniable right under international law to protect the public interest through reasonable government action. In the case of Indigenous peoples, different sources of authority demand effective actions in favor of this protected category of rightsholders. Though measures to protect the rights of Indigenous peoples *domestically* will no doubt be challenged, the unique recognition of Indigenous peoples by international law as politically vulnerable and economically marginalized justifies broad efforts to protect Indigenous peoples – in effect enlarging states' policy, regulatory or police space. Moreover, international economic institutions have offered a more expansive interpretive approach to relevant flexibilities included in treaty texts. Institutions like the WTO have drawn an actual connection to the concerns of Indigenous peoples, effectively reading those concerns as a potentially suitable justification. Similarly, in the investment terrain, recent decisions have recognized the duty of governments to protect against human rights violations and the potential contributory role of multinational corporations. This recognition, I argue, expands the capacity to utilize international economic law as a *shield* for the protection of indigenous rights.

Less effective is the use of international economic law to develop the social, economic, or cultural activities of Indigenous people. With some caveats, this possibility is also available, especially in trade and investment regimes. And while international finance safeguards are protective in nature, their presence has arguably triggered the inclusion of indigenous interests in financing and "development" programs – opening economic opportunities, one may hope, for indigenous groups. All this is caveated by the fact that to advance their interests, Indigenous peoples must sustain an active role in setting standards, safeguarding regulatory autonomy and maintaining constant representation before domestic authorities. In addition, with the judicialization of these fields, strategic litigation becomes much more relevant to test the limits of legal obligations; promote a sensible relationship between treaties; and expand the flexibilities included in legal instruments. Access to legal and policymaking expertise is therefore particularly critical for the defense or advancement of indigenous interests in an interconnected world.

There is another, more hopeful aspect. The relationship goes both ways and the analysis also shows that indigenous rights are transforming the field – for the better. As I explain there is evidence of three potentially transformational impacts that could serve as a (broad) guide for the improvement of international economic frameworks at a disruptive time. These three impacts are: (1) the incorporation of new standards, metrics and tools available in international economic treaties; (2) the modification of the practice of international economic lawmaking; and (3) the use of international economic arrangements to lock in social and economic policy for vulnerable and/or marginalized populations.

A New Path: Indigenous Peoples As Core Participants of Globalization

The last two chapters formulate proposals for actions to improve the way in which the field of international law addresses the claims and concerns of marginalized communities. In Chapter 6, I make some basic recommendations. These recommendations are only partial; they are insufficient to address the current wave of discontent with globalization's negative effects or the deep existing structural inequities between and within countries – especially as the global pandemic resulting from Covid-19 exacerbates them. But, within the realm of limited possibilities, there is incremental change and I believe deeply that the relative success of Indigenous peoples shows precisely that over time, change can happen. "They teach the importance of "resistance from within" – the development, use and importation of human rights norms, concepts and strategies into frameworks used to address economic interdependence."

The recommendations include four basic idea: (1) the idea that governing structures must, to the extent possible, include representatives of marginalized groups in the upstream and downstream law production processes – that is, in treaty negotiations and international dispute settlement proceedings; (2) the idea of using international economic agreements to give special treatment to indigenous communities and to force legal reform through them; (3) the idea that international economic law should have a basic commitment to democracy; and (4) the idea that international economic agreements should include more provisions that condition economic benefits on the implementation of processes for fair compensation and direct sharing of benefits.

Finally, in Chapter 7, I reengage with the debate over the discontents of globalization. This chapter has a twofold objective. First, I seek to highlight some of the systemic elements of disempowerment often ignored in the main "narratives" over the negative effects of globalization. Second, I seek to provide a critique more consistent with the main argument of this book. To that end, the book concludes by advocating the incorporation of indigenous perspectives in debates about the future of international economic law, including: (a) respect for distinct beliefs about and forms of economic organizations; (b) active commitment with communal self-determination; and (c) recognition of individual and corporate duties toward our planet and future generations. These, I believe, are the three most powerful insights that international economic law has failed to understand by leaving Indigenous peoples at the margins of globalization.

1

Globalization and Its Multiple Discontents

The election of President Donald Trump, which followed an indecisive vote by the citizens of the United Kingdom to leave the European Union, evidenced a deep crisis. Among others, this crisis reflects a lack of democratic support to, and appetite for projects that aim to increase economic interdependence. Old and new perspectives on this issue joined forces against a shared, common enemy – the distrust of the process often referred to as globalization.

Perspectives critical of the process of globalization are by no means new. For centuries, groups disfavored by the destabilizing forces that such processes entail, such as competition or new forms of social and business organization, or that see in it the formalization of power structures have attempted sometimes successfully to organize and protect against economic interdependence.[1] Trade policy has international but also domestic distributional effects that affect interests and prospects. Notably, however, the events of 2016 are qualitatively different as they signaled a deep division and generalized mistrust even in countries that have substantially benefited – at least from a macroeconomic perspective – from the post-World War II consensus and the neoliberal institutions that followed the fall of the Berlin Wall.[2] The once vibrant middle classes, which were propelled in part by industrialization in many Western countries, frustrated with grim perspectives about their future joined other popular and populist movements. Many of these critics pointed at (neo)economic liberalism as the culprit.

---

[1]   See Robert E. Litan, *The "Globalization" Challenge: The U.S. Role in Shaping World Trade and Investment*, BROOKINGS, Mar. 1, 2000, visit https://www.brookings.edu/articles/the-globalization-challenge-the-u-s-role-in-shaping-world-trade-and-investment.

[2]   See Robert Kuttner, *Neoliberalism: Political Success, Economic Failure*, THE AMERICAN PROSPECT, June 25, 2019, visit https://prospect.org/economy/neoliberalism-political-success-economic-failure.

In their view, this form of internationalization promotes nothing but a form of regressive redistribution – a way of making the rich even richer. Many of those disaffected chose to vote for candidates with nationalistic tendencies and, in some cases, racist undertones.[3]

To a large extent, this grim perspective that led to our current crisis of trust is not an incorrect perspective of one (among many other) effect of globalization. The interconnection of markets has facilitated the large accumulation of capital for a few with the skills, social networks and political access to participate in the global financing, servicing, trading or investing with limited constraints (compared with prior periods of humanity) – leaving many behind. It has facilitated the underinvestment in key areas that helped to underpin social cohesion, while motivating enormous dislocations of workers. At the same time, in some places more than others, globalization is perceived as the continuation of colonization that exacerbated the existing inequalities between nations. For instance, UN bodies have declared that it is necessary to contribute to the current debate to defend the interest of all and to move away from the hegemony of the major powers. Colonialism has returned under a new guise.[4] In addition, in many countries, governments have been unable or unwilling to sufficiently address these well-known effects with the adoption of policies to protect the disaffected – for instance, with retraining programs, the expansion of the social safety net or increasing access to affordable healthcare and education. To make things even worse, the volatility of intensely interconnected economies also made traditionally stable societies much more vulnerable to recurrent systemic exogenous shocks and, as seen in recent months, susceptible to epidemics.[5]

More problematically, the responses to the cyclical crises have had – sometimes by design – the effect of benefiting the same sophisticated, wealthy or already empowered actors who can insulate from volatility and take advantage of bailouts and other rescue programs *with a tilt*. Take, for instance, the effects of the policy responses to the financial crisis of 2008: despite its potentially beneficial effects that may have avoided disastrous consequences

3   See Ronald F. Inglehart & Pippa Norris, *Trump, Brexit, and the Rise of Populism: Economic Have-Nots and Cultural Backlash*, HARVARD KENNEDY SCHOOL, FACULTY RESEARCH WORKING PAPER SERIES, Aug. 2016, visit https://research.hks.harvard.edu/publications/getFile .aspx?Id=1401.

4   See United Nations, *Impact of Globalization on Various Areas of World Discussed by Heads of UN Regional Commissions*, Feb. 14, 2000, visit https://www.un.org/press/en/2000/20000214 .tad1908.doc.html.

5   Monica Potts, *The American Social Safety Net Does Not Exist*, THE NATION, Oct. 13, 2016, visit https://www.thenation.com/article/archive/the-american-social-safety-net-does-not-exist.

of the economic downfall, it also allowed a deeper concentration of economic power by wealthy citizens who disproportionally benefited from the eventual recovery of the markets. Incidentally, no one was made accountable for the reckless behavior of many in the financial services industry who contributed to the crisis. Instead, the blame was directed to exogenous factors.

But these very same concerns with globalization predated the election of Trump and Brexit – in fact, if anything these criticisms are recurrent. Back in the 1990s it was suggested that the increase in the gap between rich and poor in wealthy nations due to globalization would motivate protests against the excessive reliance on free market ideas.[6] More importantly, many poor nations and constituencies within them have long taken issue and criticized the pace and form of globalization, as it gives them increasingly fewer prospects to succeed. What the recurrent criticism of economic integration shows is that rather than one big problem of globalization, there are multiple problematic effects (as well as real benefits). Depending where one stands, globalization can be framed differently.[7]

This book is concerned mainly with one particular frame; that of the groups subjugated and marginalized by the process of globalization. As I explain, Indigenous peoples, whose voices have been until recently excluded in international economic institutions represent an example of how modern economic interconnection can marginalize millions. Their perspective and experience may also provide a path for organizing transformative action. To contextualize the discussion, it is important to situate the perspective on globalization of these groups in opposition to others, or as Anthea Roberts and Nicolas Lamp say, as the different narratives driving debates about who wins and loses in modern times.[8] Accordingly, the different views of globalization can be organized in six main "narratives" – five of them seek to contest the process, in one form or another, by relying on particular goals as well as tools, standards and metrics to assess success. Each framing reveals and obscures different elements about the relative "winners" and "losers" of economic globalization; each has a particular perspective of how we should respond to the current crises. Nevertheless, without a holistic approach to the

---

[6] See generally CAROLINE THOMAS & PETER WILKIN, GLOBALIZATION AND THE SOUTH (Springer 1997).

[7] Noah Smith, *The Dark Side of Globalization: Why Seattle's 1999 Protesters Were Right*, THE ATLANTIC, Jan. 6, 2014, visit https://www.theatlantic.com/business/archive/2014/01/the-dark-side-of-globalization-why-seattles-1999-protesters-were-right/282831.

[8] Nicolas Lamp, *How Should We Think about the Winners and Losers from Globalization? Three Narratives and Their Implications for the Redesign of International Economic Agreements*, 30 EJIL 1359 (2019).

different perspectives on the discontents of globalization and given that all of the narratives reveal problematic aspects of globalization, it would be partial and misleading to address the issue of the marginalized without this context as a starting point of reference.

What follows is a summary of the type of orthodoxy that has animated most modern trade and investment frameworks with IP provisions such as the WTO Agreements, ASEAN Free Trade Agreement, NAFTA (or its updated version, the USMCA) and the now uncertain TPP (or CP-TPP) and Trans-Atlantic Trade and Investment Partnership (TTIP) agreements, as well as many other similar deals. After that, I juxtapose the frames identified by Lamp and Roberts, adding commentary to complement this initial picture of where we are in this historical movement.

1.1 GLOBALIZATION AND ABSOLUTE GAINS

The conventional or mainstream narrative is a perspective widely adopted by economists as well as international economic law scholars and policymakers in developed Western countries such as the United States, Europe and the United Kingdom. In a largely simplified fashion, it argues – based on some often disputed or conflicting empirical evidence – that globalization increases the prospects of both peace and prosperity. First, it increases economic prosperity because measures aimed at restricting trade in goods and services as well as foreign direct investment limit economic efficiency. Hence, contracting at the international level is necessary to avoid inefficiencies. In the long run, this has the effect of increasing absolute gains on at least a national level, even if such benefits are not evenly distributed among the different constituencies of the state. By removing tariffs and other barriers, states can focus on what they do best and improve their economic standing. Specialization plus economies of scale allows the commercial actors of a given state to trade for other products with greater economic returns. This perspective claims that economic liberalization is a path for economic development; it points to the experiences of countries in South East Asia as instructive examples of the virtues of the model.

At the margins, under this narrative there is some degree of disagreement on the effects of economic globalization and, more importantly, what to do about it. On the one side, neoliberal conservatives tend to believe strongly in the market; they often focuses on the state as the culprit of multiple inefficiencies. This is often considered the "right" or conservative wing of the political spectrum in many countries, including the United States and the United Kingdom. On the other side, many accept that markets indeed maximize

economic gains in the long term, but view the state as playing a more fundamental role in regulating markets (including short-term opportunism), redistributing those gains and providing an effective safety net. This view is more akin
to social democratic perspectives in Continental Europe, where the social
welfare state has a stronger tradition and defends broader policy interventions.[9]
While this view also embraces international economic liberalization as a
path for economic development, it demands greater redistribution and social
services to cushion the negative impacts of economic globalization on the
national level.

Second, and regardless of one's position on its economic effects, interdependence was first and foremost assumed to increase the prospects for peace and
security. Peace and security are public goods – perhaps the main and most
valuable outcome of international law. This goal was particularly relevant
during the foundation of the Bretton Woods institutions, that is, the World
Bank, the IMF and the failed International Trade Organization, which eventually emerged in the form of the WTO. The theory is simple and perhaps has
even less methodical empirical support than the economic role of the system,
but defends greater economic interdependence as a way to promote cooperation and increase the costs of conflict. The focus is on the absolute gains of
states, including peace, so that it makes sense for them to engage in free trade on
an individual basis, with much less attention paid to the size or proportion of
their gains on a relative basis. In other words, overall countries are better off in
absolute terms, and therefore less inclined to engage in destructive conflict.

Beneath these general arguments, however, different positions have been
gaining force among different sectors of the population, especially in Western
democracies. What separates these positions from the mainstream perspective
is a different understanding on how to assess the effects of globalization. These
positions mainly focus on the relative effects: Some individuals or collectivities
win, and others lose. Before explaining other, more radical positions that
argue that perhaps everyone loses from the relentless quest for economic
growth, I explain four different challenges to conventional economic thought
and how each is different from the others.

1.2 DISCONTENTS BASED ON RELATIVE GAINS

For many years, the conventional view of globalization has had different
pushback from scholars, advocates and civil society organizations. Relying

---

[9] ANDREW GLYN, SOCIAL DEMOCRACY IN NEOLIBERAL TIMES: THE LEFT AND ECONOMIC
POLICY SINCE 1980 (Oxford University Press 2001).

on different perspectives and metrics, these actors have contested globalization not necessarily challenging the paradigm of absolute gains, but by highlighting the relative gains that globalization often enables. In this sense, depending on the perspective, actors have framed the conversation as a matter of relative gains: who has won at the expense of whom. Because of the temporal effects of economic liberalization, many of the claims are hard to evaluate empirically.

Certainly, as these narratives care about relative gains, the important issue here is what each reveals about globalization. No narrative is infallible or completely accurate, but there is some level of truth in all of them. Nevertheless, the narratives are often presented in a decontextualized fashion and weaponize the more intuitive or salient aspects of each narrative for political gains. Not surprisingly, the use of the relative effects of globalization to animate different political causes has been a constant, as I now explain with reference to Lamp and Roberts' topology.

1.2.1 *The Populist Discontent*

Globalization has been challenged from a populist perspective for many years, but such challenges intensified in the United States after the Global Financial Crisis of 2008 and the bailout provided by the federal government to "Wall Street" – banks and financial institutions which failed to assess, or decided to ignore, the systemic risks that their activities entailed.[10] In Europe it coincided with the Greek crisis and the debate about its mismanagement and the role of Germany and its banks. The economic "system," according to this perspective, is "rigged" and mostly benefits the top 1 percent. This 1 percent represents millionaires and billionaires who have a disproportionate influence in the local domestic political process and routinely meet in places like Davos or Dubai to find ways to increase their wealth, including by avoiding a fair contribution to domestic economies and paying taxes.

The disproportionate gains by a concentrated group raise concerns about fairness. For example, left-to-center politicians like senators Bernie Sanders or Elizabeth Warren, utilize the effects (whether real or perceived) of globalization on income distribution to advocate its retrenchment or transformation.[11] As it is, and in coordination with domestic political processes, globalization

---

[10] Thomas A. Russo & Aaron J. Katzel, The 2008 Financial Crisis and Its Aftermath: Addressing the Next Debt Challenge (Group of Thirty: Washington, DC, 2011).

[11] Andrew Soergel, *Study: Globalization Has Boosted Income Inequality*, U.S. News & World Report (May 2017), visit https://www.usnews.com/news/articles/2017-05-08/globalization-boosted-income-inequality-study-says.

reflects another instance of how the rules of the game have been rigged to benefit the wealthy few at the expense of the many poor. The evidence, including a compelling and detailed description of the relative gains that have resulted in the last few decades provided by Thomas Piketty, a Nobel Prize-winning economist, has helped to reposition versions of this view at the center of policy discussions, including among academicians.

The conventional counterargument to this perspective is that it is for national governments to address the adverse consequences of globalization, which enables a temporal process ... sectors and facilitates the accumulation ... (winner takes all). Hence, fair taxation, social programs and well-regulated markets can address issues like stagnant wages or wealth concentration. Moreover, it behooves governments to address the rising cost of the essentials for the middle class like education, healthcare and housing. Globalization can do little to address these problems – although governments have defended conditioning trade deals to a commitment to such policies as I explain in the next section. Not surprisingly, these arguments have done little to ease the concerns espoused by the populist frame.

1.2.2 *The Corporate Power Discontent*

Similarly, some believe that the gains from globalization flow disproportionately to the richest individuals who control transnational corporations. This view stresses the role of corporate (or capital) power versus "Main Street" (or labor) interests and has a transnational dimension. It sees international economic treaties combined with a suboptimal international tax, competition and regulatory regimes as the cause or as an enabler of international corporate power.[12] By doing so, corporations can take advantage of a global marketplace to produce cheaply, sell everywhere and avoid paying their fair share of taxes without much competition.

Under this view, the network of international trade, tax, investment and IP treaties facilitate the free flow of goods, services and capital but make footloose and flexible multinational companies hardly accountable. Because of the lack of commitment to social inclusion – critics argue – these treaties allow governments and workers to play off each other, leading to what is often referred to as social dumping.[13] If workers in Michigan do not lower their

---

[12] Alex Cobham, *Could the World Trade Organization See a Challenge to Tax Havenry?* TAX JUSTICE NETWORK (July 2018), visit https://www.taxjustice.net/2018/07/04/why-wto-tax-havens.

[13] Gregory Shaffer, *Retooling Trade Agreements for Social Inclusion*, 2019 U. ILL. L. REV. 1 (2019).

wage demands, the automaker can move production to San Luis Potosi in Mexico. It also may lead to regulatory and tax arbitrage – if taxes are too high, or regulations too onerous, companies may relocate headquarters or production.

The counterargument to this framing of globalization is similar to that against the populist critique, with some caveats. Globalization depends on a responsible center-right partner to succeed. Policies that underpin a functioning liberal system are premised on the understanding that at least a faction of policymakers would be willing to support market-friendly ideas that address the negative consequences of globalization, including job loss, temporal shocks and a rise in inequality. Yet, the role of money in politics, not globalization, is directly to blame for the lack of action in making corporations more accountable (although the two can be connected). In this sense, corporate power has disproportionate effects on political discourse and has helped to polarize it. Some might also argue that overall, global interconnectedness improves the labor and regulatory conditions and the overall distribution of wealth as measured by objective indicators such as the Gini index. Accordingly, looking at corporate accumulation misses the point without a clearer picture of how globalization affects more concrete metrics such as inequality and social mobility, especially compared with other forms of organization.

1.2.3 *The Protectionist Discontent*

The protectionist view focuses on the relative gains but differs in a fundamental way from the previous narratives. Like the populist view, this perspective challenges globalization from the perspective of a particular set of "losers" of the process, that is, individual citizens.[14] However, unlike the populist view, this is not necessarily the poor or the middle class, but rather those workers from post-industrial communities who have lost their jobs to newly developed manufacturing centers, with sometimes devastating consequences for their communities. Because in countries such as the United States or the United Kingdom these workers resemble traditionally economic dominant groups such as white males, in some instances the narrative has adopted a xenophobic and/or racist undertone. Think, for instance, of the United Kingdom and the Brexit vote or the United States and the election of President Trump.

---

[14] Dani Rodrik, *Populism and the Economics of Globalization*, J. INT. BUS. (2018) Vol. 1, 12–33.

Under the protectionist narrative, workers in developing countries such as China, Vietnam or Mexico – just to mention a few – or immigrants, who may be willing to work harder for less money, are the main beneficiaries of globalization. They fault developing countries for using unfair trade practices to "steal" jobs or accuse governments of not enforcing harsh immigration laws. Like the populist narrative, for the protectionist the "elites" are complicit in allowing imbalanced trade and investment deals that result in job losses.

Several counterarguments are advanced against this view of globalization. Most prominently, defenders of globalization point to a different cause of job losses: the efficiency gains resulting from better integrated supply chains as well as automatization. It is the robots, not Mexican or Polish workers who are the ones to blame. In addition, a standard response puts the blame on the lack of mechanisms of redistribution such as retraining programs, or safety nets or healthcare expansions as the culprits of the negative effects of globalization. Perhaps one benefit of this protectionist view is that it has opened space to question strict economic considerations and for perspectives that pay greater heed to the social consequences of globalization.[15]

1.2.4 *The Geoeconomic Discontent*

A fourth perspective similarly challenges the relative gains that seem to flow to different countries. However, this narrative is less concerned with the fate of individual workers, like the protectionist view, but instead focuses on the unequal gains that different countries have made through economic globalization. Under this focus, the gains of some countries, especially China, are considered a threat to national security. Therefore, trade policies demand measures that seek to expand flexibility, policy space or discretion to implement trade measures to protect the industrial and manufacturing base on national security grounds. Investment policies require increased screening of foreign investment in critical infrastructure, and to impose new export constraints with respect to key, cutting-edge technologies.

This "geoeconomic" narrative is rapidly emerging as the economic emergence of China is perceived as a threat to an American-led world. This can result in a more autonomous (though still competitive) "spheres of influence" approach, in which trade policy is deployed to further strategic goals and to force other nations to pick a side similar to the Cold War era. The perspective from absolute to relative gains is particularly marked. Advocates for this view

---

[15] Richard Baldwin, The Globotics Upheaval: Globalization, Robotics and the Future of Work (Oxford University Press 2019).

do not question that most countries have gained from economic globalization; instead, the concern seems to be with the disproportionate gains of China compared to the United States, Europe and others. In particular, the concern is that the strength of China might endanger other countries' access to vital resources and control over critical infrastructure, resulting in the undermining of "Western" power and "liberal" values.

The response to this narrative is only emerging but is similar to economic arguments against claims taken based on "national security" or national interest. In essence, the response argues that interconnected nations tend to engage in less (not more) conflict, as the mutual losses become increasingly costly. This view stresses that national security aspects of interconnection are the main reasons for more (not less) globalization. In part, the arguments for the The Comprehensive and Progressive Agreement for Trans-Pacific Partnership (TPP or **CPTPP**), and many FTAs signed by the United States included a strong national security component. When advancing these arguments, the public is often reminded of the success of endeavors, such as the EU, that have a national security perspective and have worked well to prevent a repetition of conflicts such as World War II.

All these forms of contestation to the standard narrative are used to advance different causes – and with that economic and political interests. For example, in the United States, Senators Sanders and Warren used the populist and corporate power narratives to create a coalition of voters (ultimately unsuccessful) and to appeal to labor organizations. Similarly, President Trump used and continues to rely on the geoeconomic and protectionist views to expand national security powers.[16] Different economic actors also espouse these views – more traditional industries like coal or steel use the protectionist view to benefit from subsidization or tariffs, and newer industries like high tech rely on the geoeconomic narrative to undermine their foreign competitors. The targeting of Huawei Technologies Co., China's largest tech company, by the United States is instructive because it benefits other Western companies interested in dominating a new generation of wireless systems.

It is also interesting to note that none of these perspectives directly espouses the interests of groups that suffer from political marginalization and economic vulnerability such as indigenous groups. Even the most populist views seem to be distant from the perspective of groups left out by the dynamics of globalization, who are politically unable to advance their concerns and are

---

[16] Ana Swanson & Paul Mozur, *Trump Mixes Economic and National Security, Plunging the U.S. into Multiple Fights*, N.Y. TIMES, June 8, 2019, visit https://www.nytimes.com/2019/06/08/business/trump-economy-national-security.html.

marginalized from participating economically. This has led some indigenous movements to align more directly with radical perspectives, including the sustainability and 'Third World' perspectives. In Chapter 7, I come back to this issue to explain a perspective of globalization that is more consistent with the rights, interests and grievances of Indigenous peoples. First however, I explain this sustainability narrative and why indigenous advocates have not completely embraced this perspective.

1.3 DISCONTENTS BASED ON ABSOLUTE LOSSES

1.3.1 *The Sustainability Perspective*

For many years different perspectives have challenged the market-driven, consumption-based and economic growth paradigms that underpin the current model of globalization, especially as understood by orthodox neoliberals.[17] These more fundamental challenges do not focus on the relative effects, but on the absolute ones. There are two related arguments. First, the main focus of globalization should be sustainability of the planet and the well-being of all planetary living forms and the development of human capabilities, not just economic growth. Instead, the current model puts the planet at peril for it rewards commoditization and unsustainable exploitation of natural resources and disregards the perilous consequences of excessive pollution. Second, the model also incentivizes unreasonable accumulation as well as a "winner takes all" logic that tends to exacerbate inequality – for example, today, eight people have the same wealth as the billions in the poorest half of the world's population. In the long run, this increased inequality means that everyone loses as it tends to make society worse off, not just those who are relatively worse off in economic terms. Without a middle class, social mobility and basic social safety nets, societal connections breakdown, potentially dissipating the fabrics of society that prevent conflict. This dynamic – in the long run – affects most, if not all members of society.

This position is often adopted by environmental and social and economic justice movements. Instead of prioritizing economic growth, this lens often argues for different metrics of individual and societal well-being. It advocates measures that focus on equality, healthier (mental and physical) lives and an optimal use of resources, expressing an expansive (and perhaps more realistic)

---

[17] ORG. FOR ECON. CO-OPERATION & DEV., Report of the Secretary General's Advisory Group on a New Growth Narrative *Beyond Growth: Towards a New Economic Approach*, Sept. 12, 2019.

idea of externalities that impact the balance of the planet. It pushes back against the most unsustainable forms of international interconnectedness that disregard the long-term effects on the planet, even in cases that show positive effects.

The most effective counterargument is that perhaps in no other time in history have more people been taken out of poverty than in the last forty years or so. Despite the deep problems, we are living in a time of remarkable progress and achievements in combating poverty, especially in the developing world. China alone has been responsible for a large number of these people who now have much better options in terms of health, education and well-being. While the world is at peril because of environmental practices, they have improved substantially and societies have also become more productive and efficient, especially compared with any other time in history. One example is that despite the climate change challenge, the carbon emissions per unit of global GDP improves daily and we are learning to resolve challenges that used to be fatal for societies. These challenges can only be resolved with global interconnected action, where markets can be part of the solution, and not in isolation and excluding efficient forms of organization.

1.3.2 *TWAIL and Other Perspectives*

There are many other perspectives that resemble the sustainability approach. An important one may be expressed by *critical globalization studies*, law and development scholars, as well as scholars under the umbrella of Third World approaches to international law (TWAIL).[18] Unlike others, they emphasize continuity between colonial times and the current wave of globalization; they do not see a radical rupture with past forms of economic integration but a continuation that has formalized preexisting relationships and forms of oppressions existent during prior historical Eras such as mercantilism, colonialism and feudalism.

While these perspectives emphasize the struggle between social classes, they also identify globalization as a way of perpetuating the power of North Atlantic countries by empowering unaccountable transnational business entities, and a global "super class." The result is the alienation of communities that do not abide by a culture of individual choice; one that glorifies the efficiency of markets or the role of privately held property, including communities in the "Third World" or "Global South." Some of these perspectives

---

[18] James Gathii, *Imperialism, Colonialism, and International Law*, 54 BUFF. L. R. 1013 (2007).

also adopt a racially charged undertone, but fail to define which groups are the subjugated communities. Accordingly, modern international economic frameworks only serve to maintain a racialized system, privileging white, North Atlantic communities.

One problem is that some of these perspectives tend to be pessimistic and rarely engage with traditional measures, empiricism or indicators of the impact of globalization. At the rhetoric level, some scholars tend to see such indicators as biased or as technologies of governance that ignore the realities and perspectives of communities outside traditional power structures. For instance, law and development scholars contest the meaning of "development" as a politically charged term that dismisses the preferences and practices of poor countries.[19] To some degree, the emphasis of politics make these approaches less effective to perform objective, empirical evaluations. The response, however, is similar to the sustainability narrative but given the lack of engagement with more specific metrics they are also more readily dismissed, often for lacking concrete proposals of change.

* * *

As I elaborate in Chapter 7, the main criticisms of globalization fail to capture fully the interests of Indigenous peoples. On the one hand, the challenges based on relative gains rarely include the perspective of Indigenous peoples or take into account the experiences of these communities in their arguments. In general, these perspectives completely ignore both the specific protections of Indigenous peoples and the ways in which these groups can effectively participate by integrating into a cosmopolitan community more welcoming of these experiences – often assuming that, as the relative losers, they are uninterested in incremental change and participation. This needs not be true for all indigenous groups.

On the other hand, perspectives based on absolute losses have been adopted by indigenous advocates who argue for systemic change, but fail to grasp fully this group's interests. The sustainability perspective often disregards the interest of indigenous groups of participating in the gradual exploitation of their territories and resources. For instance, a large percentage of the remaining (yet, rapidly disappearing) healthy ecosystems in the world are indigenous lands, and the sustainability perspective sees indigenous communities as bearers of the responsibility to keep them protected from economic activity

---

[19] Jeswald W. Salacuse, *From Developing Countries to Emerging Markets: A Changing Role for Law in the Third World*, 33 Int'l L 875 (1999) https://scholar.smu.edu/til/vol33/iss4/5.

and generally untouched. This approach effectively advocates for the conservation of indigenous resources, without regard to the autonomy, priorities, desires or aspirations of such communities. Indigenous people, the argument seems to imply, should not be aspiring to be economic participants and bargain with these resources to set some of the terms, but instead should act as the protectors of the ecosystems for the benefit of all of us (especially tourists) – no matter if this means their continuous marginalization.

Finally, the sustainability perspective assumes certain level of political participation and influence. In most cases such political participation is nonexistent or, if any, very limited. Conversely, the critical perspective tends to ignore the special protections of Indigenous peoples reflected in human rights instruments. In fact, Indigenous peoples have had, not without sharp resistance, extensive opportunities to participate in shaping the development of the modern human rights system that has emerged along with this new wave of globalization. By completely ignoring these victories, the critical perspective fails to bring into the fold the special protections that apply to them as marginalized groups. In Chapter 3, I discuss how these protections operate after systematically explaining the negative effects of globalization on marginalized groups such as Indigenous peoples.

2

The Process of Susceptibility and Exclusion

The global ascendancy of neoliberal economics has deepened inequalities between and within nations and largely undermined efforts toward sustainable development.[1] Based on a belief that *the market* should be the organizing principle for social, political and economic decisions, policymakers in many countries promoted privatization of state activities and an increased role for the free market, flexibility in labor markets and trade and investment liberalization.[2] The benefits of these policies frequently fail to reach the Indigenous peoples of the world, who acutely feel their costs, such as environmental degradation, cultural dispossessions and loss of traditional lands and territories.[3]

As vulnerable and often marginalized segments of the world's population, Indigenous peoples are at a heightened risk of experiencing the negative consequences of globalization. Understanding this reality could provide pathways for effective interventions to alleviate, overcome or at the very least, minimize such effects.[4] For the most part, these negative effects result from the diminished ability of Indigenous peoples to enjoy the widely documented

---

[1] UNITED NATIONS DEPARTMENT OF ECONOMIC AND SOCIAL AFFAIRS, STATE OF THE WORLD'S INDIGENOUS PEOPLES (New York: United Nations, 2009) at 16.

[2] *Id.*

[3] *Id.*

[4] See Committee on the Elimination of Racial Discrimination ("CERD"), *Concluding Observations on the Combined Twenty-Second and Twenty-Third Periodic Reports of Peru*, ¶ 15, U.N. Doc. CERD/C/PER/CO/22–23 (May 23, 2018); CERD, *Concluding Observations on the Combined Initial and Second to Fifth Periodic Reports of Honduras*, ¶ 20, U.N. Doc. CERD/C/HND/CO/1-5 (Mar. 13, 2014); CERD, *Concluding Observations on Belize, Adopted by the Committee under the Review Procedure at Its Eighty-First Session* (Aug. 6–13, 2012), ¶ 10, U.N. Doc. CERD/C/BLZ/CO/1 (May 3, 2013); see also Comm. on Econ., Social and Cultural Rights, *Concluding Observations on the Initial Report of Indonesia*, ¶ 39, U.N. Doc. E/C.12/IDN/CO/1 (June 19, 2014); Human Rights Comm., *Concluding Observations on Belize in the Absence of a Report, Adopted by the Committee at Its 107th Session* (March 11–28, 2013), ¶ 25, U.N. Doc. CCPR/C/BLZ/CO/1 (Apr. 26, 2013); Olivier De Schutter (Special Rapporteur on the Right to Food), *Mission to Cameroon*, ¶ 47, U.N.

benefits of economic interdependence, mainly a large increase in global trade and investment and rapid economic development.[5] In some cases and under certain conditions, indigenous groups can substantially improve their standing (think, for instance, of the Seminole Tribe of Florida that expanded its Hard Rock cafe, hotel and casino business around the world thanks to the same process of globalization).[6] The general conditions of some indigenous groups have also improved in absolute terms in recent times as a consequence of economic interdependence.[7] Yet a lot more remains to be done.

To have a productive conversation about how best to advance their general interests in the current international legal context, it is important to understand and acknowledge how international economic law, in its promotion of ideas like efficiency, innovation, freedom and entrepreneurship, creates or exacerbates systemic challenges for Indigenous peoples. Other populations, such as women, people with disabilities and national and ethnic minorities, suffer similar challenges (that should also be thoroughly explored), but globalization is particularly unforgiving for Indigenous peoples – hence, my focus in this book. For example, Indigenous peoples face special threats to their environment, cultural heritage and ability to access medicines, as well as general threats to their economic and social well-being, when some foreign investors obtain the right to extract, exploit, and export raw materials.[8]

Doc. A/HRC/22/50/Add.2 (Dec. 18, 2012); CERD, *Consideration of Reports Submitted by States Parties under Article 9 of the Convention*, U.N. Doc. CERD/C/GUY/CO/14 (Apr. 4, 2006).

[5] Comm'n on Human Rights, *Review of Developments Pertaining to the Promotion and Protection of Human Rights and Fundamental Freedoms of Indigenous People*, U.N. Doc. E/CN.4/Sub.2/AC.4/2003/2, at 4 (June 16, 2003), https://www.refworld.org/pdfid/3f4f6c2b4.pdf ("Indigenous peoples particularly tend to be left out of the benefits of globalization at the political, economic and social levels. They are often excluded from political life, as they lack adequate political participation and self-representation. Moreover, they often suffer from economic inequalities reflected in the lack of access to productive assets, services and opportunities").

[6] Lauren Gensler, *An Alligator Wrestler, a Casino Boss and a $12 Billion Tribe*, FORBES (Oct. 19, 2016), https://www.forbes.com/sites/laurengensler/2016/10/19/seminole-tribe-florida-hard-rock-cafe/#456d2f105bbc.

[7] See, e.g., Daniel R. Faber & Deborah McCarthy, *Neo-liberalism, Globalization and the Struggle for Ecological Democracy: Linking Sustainability and Environmental Justice*, in JUST SUSTAINABILITIES: DEVELOPMENT IN AN UNEQUAL WORLD 38, 50 (Julian Agyeman et al. eds., 2003); MARK NUTTALL, PROTECTING THE ARCTIC: INDIGENOUS PEOPLES AND CULTURAL SURVIVAL 53–6 (1998); Megan Davis, *Preliminary Observations: Indigenous Australia and the Australia-United States Free Trade Agreement*, 2 NGIYA: TALK L. 76, 80–1 (2008).

[8] See generally Fons Coomans, *The Ogoni Case before the African Commission on Human and Peoples' Rights*, 52 INT. COMP. LAW Q. 3, 749–760 (2003). There are positive trends on the protection of the environment by FTAs as I explain shortly; see, e.g., Canada-Colombia Free Trade Agreement, chapter 17, visit https://www.international.gc.ca/trade-commerce/trade-agreements-accords-commerciaux/agr-acc/colombia-colombie/fta-ale/17.aspx?lang=eng.

They face similar threats when trade liberalization in sectors like textiles results in the relocation of production or the increase in competition.[9] Some authors locate the root of the problem not in international economic law but in international law itself, as it tends to exclude Indigenous peoples "from its distribution of sovereign power and [include] them within the sovereign power of states established on the territories they had inhabited."[10]

Before explaining how different fields deal with the particular protections that international law provides indigenous populations, it is important to dissect the general systemic effects that the modern forms of globalization – mainly, modern trade and investment frameworks with IP provisions like the WTO Agreements, ASEAN Free Trade Agreement, NAFTA (or USMCA) and the now uncertain TPP (or CP-TPP) and Trans-Atlantic Trade and Investment Partnership ("TTIP") agreements – have on Indigenous peoples. To facilitate its understanding, I term these effects, taken together, "the cycle of susceptibility and exclusion." As a useful heuristic, I use a diagram to explain the "cycle" that results from the interaction of four processes that cause related but distinct negative systemic consequences, both direct and indirect harms. Such harms can be political (a lack of input legitimacy and participation and a shift in governance priorities) or economic (discrimination and a rise in inequality). The *cycle* can be simplified and visualized as follows:

TABLE 2.1[11] *The susceptibility and exclusion framework*

	Political	Economic
Direct	Illegitimacy	Discrimination
Indirect	Reregulation	Inequality

---

9   See *IACHR: Demands on Indigenous Consultation to Ratify Free Trade Agreements*, IWGIA (Dec. 15, 2016), visit https://www.iwgia.org/en/panama/2474-iachr-demands-on-indigenous-consultation-to-ratify.

10 Patrick Macklem, *Human Rights in International Law: Three Generations or One?* 3 LONDON REV. INT'L. L. 61, 89 (2015). For a different, see Benedict Kingsbury, *Whose International Law? Sovereignty and Non-state Groups*, 88 AM. SOC'Y OF INT'L L. PROC. 1, 1 (1994).

11 Sergio Puig, *International Indigenous Economic Law*, 52 U.C. DAVIS. L. REV. 1243, 1260 (2019).

2.1 ILLEGITIMACY

Politically, the fundamental flaw of international economic agreements is the lack of procedural and democratic legitimacy – or, input legitimacy. Indigenous peoples have had, not without sharp resistance, extensive opportunities to participate in shaping the development of the modern human rights system.[12] However, with some notable exceptions and like many other groups, they have very often been excluded from providing input and/or effectively participating in the main processes that create international economic law – including treaty negotiations and adjudicatory lawmaking before dispute settlement bodies. As explained by Thomas Poggee, "the contest over international rules and procedures is essentially confined to small elites of agents – MNCs, industry associations, banks, hedge funds, billionaires – who can effectively influence the negotiating position of the most powerful governments."[13]

Systemic barriers prevent Indigenous peoples from advancing their interests in the processes of international economic law creation.[14] State obligations grant Indigenous peoples rights to participate in public affairs,[15] but in most

[12] See United Nations Department of Economic and Social Affairs, *Indigenous Peoples Historical Overview*, visit https://www.un.org/development/desa/indigenouspeoples/declaration-on-the-rights-of-indigenous-peoples/historical-overview.html. See also CLAIRE CHARTERS & RODOLFO STAVENHAGEN (eds.) MAKING THE DECLARATION WORK: THE UNITED NATIONS DECLARATION ON THE RIGHTS OF INDIGENOUS PEOPLES (Copenhagen: IWGIA, 2009).

[13] Thomas Pogge, *International Law between Two Futures*, 5 J. INT'L. DISP. SETTLEMENT 432, 432 (2014). To be sure, indigenous groups are not the only ones effectively excluded from the process; think labor unions in many countries and the rural poor. For a decision excluding Indigenous people from investment arbitration participation, see Bernhard von Pezold v. Republic of Zim., ICSID Case No. ARB/10/15, Procedural Order No. 2, ¶ 56 (June 26, 2012) (rejecting the participation of "indigenous groups" for "apparent lack of independence or neutrality").

[14] Human Rights Council, Rep. of the Expert Mechanism on the Rights of Indigenous Peoples, ¶ 10, U.N. Doc. A/HRC/EMRIP/2011/2 (May 26, 2011) ("Mechanisms enabling the participation of Indigenous peoples ... can be problematic for various reasons").

[15] *Id.* at ¶ 3; see also Office of the High Comm'r for Human Rights, *General Comment No. 23: The Rights of Minorities (Art. 27)*, ¶ 7, U.N. Doc. CCPR/C/21/Rev.1/Add.5 (Aug. 4, 1994); Comm. on the Elimination of Racial Discrimination, *General Recommendation No. 23: Indigenous Peoples*, ¶ 4(d), U.N. Doc. A/52/18, annex V (Aug. 18, 1997) (stating "[t]he Committee calls in particular upon States parties to ... [e]nsure that members of Indigenous peoples have equal rights in respect of effective participation in public life and that no decisions directly relating to their rights and interests are taken without their informed consent"); *Demands on Indigenous Consultation, supra* note 26 ("Consultation is a requirement whenever there are issues that affect Indigenous peoples' territories, particularly in the case of extractive industry investments"). But see Hupacasath First Nation v. Minister of Foreign Affairs Can. & the Att'y Gen. of Can., [2013] 2013 F.C. 900 (Can.) (holding that Canada does not owe a duty to consult indigenous peoples before the ratification of an IIA).

instances the influence is limited by the lack of indigenous representation and decision-making processes that are tailored to their needs.[16] Very often, inadequate capacity, assistance and advice in what are by definition very technical negotiations (e.g., Technical Barriers to Trade Agreement), result in the inability of Indigenous peoples to safeguard effectively their interests.

The lack of impactful participation of Indigenous peoples in legal disputes – an avenue of crucial importance for the definition of rights and obligations under economic arrangements – is increasingly damaging. These cases occur in different dispute settlement forums ranging from the WTO[17] to the WBG's International Centre for Settlement of Investment Disputes ("ICSID").[18] Such cases show that even if Indigenous peoples have the means to present even an argument before a dispute settlement body, the argument will be influential only if a state has agreed to advance that argument, which it will not do when its own interest conflicts with that of the indigenous group. One example is an investment dispute involving tourism developments in the traditional lands of the Ngöbe-Buglé people. While the Ngöbe-Buglé were central actors within that dispute and the decision directly impacted them, they were dissuaded by Panama from presenting an *amicus* brief.[19]

---

[16] Definitely, there are positive experiences of indigenous participation in relation to standards setting. See, e.g., Navin Raj, Implementation of the World Bank's Indigenous Peoples Policy, A Learning Review (FY 2006–2008) 22 (Operational Policy & Country Servs., Working Paper No. 64757, 2011).

[17] Panel Report, *United States – Import Prohibition of Certain Shrimp and Shrimp Products*, ¶ 99, WTO Doc. WT/DS58/R (adopted May 15, 1998) (stating "[w]e note that, pursuant to Article 13 of the DSU, the initiative to seek information and to select the source of information rests with the Panel"). This position was later reversed by the Appellate Body. See Appellate Body Report, *United States – Final Countervailing Duty Determination with Respect to Certain Softwood Lumber from Canada*, WTO Doc. WT/DS257/AB/R (adopted Feb. 17, 2004) (acknowledging the receipt of an amicus brief submitted by the Indigenous Network on Economies and Trade, yet failing to address the concerns raised).

[18] See *Bernhard von Pezold, supra* note 13 at ¶ 56 (rejecting request by four indigenous groups to submit amicus curiae briefs to the tribunal); see also Glamis Gold Ltd. v. United States, Decision on Application and Submission by Quechan Indian Nation (NAFTA Arb. Trib. 2005), https://www.state .gov/documents/organization/53592.pdf (granting NAFTA investment dispute panel's request by the Quechan Indian Nation to file a submission detailing its views on the dispute, yet failing to address the concerns advanced by the Quechan Nation in its award).

[19] Álvarez y Marín Corporación S.A. y Otros c. República de Pan., ICSID Case No. ARB/15/14, Motivation of the Decision Concerning the Preliminary Objections of the Plaintiff Regarding Rule 41(5) of the ICSID Arbitration Rules, paras. 13–17 (Jan. 27, 2016); Clovis Trevino, *Panama Faces New ICSID Arbitration over Thwarted Hotel Tourism Development*, Inv. Arb. Rep., Apr. 24, 2015.

2.2 DISCRIMINATION

Economically, a negative effect of this political disenfranchisement and lack of representation, especially in treaty negotiations, is discrimination – a *de facto* disadvantage of Indigenous peoples introduced by the main goal of these frameworks. As currently understood, these frameworks attempt to level the playing field between products, services and investments of foreigners and nationals. This continues the vicious circle: As a result of existing barriers to participation on the part of Indigenous peoples, international economic arrangements further erode their bargaining position and ability to advance their economic interests in the newly created international markets.

Certainly, trade and investment treaties concluded by states, or financing agreements between states and international financial institutions, can create new markets, economic opportunities for entire countries, and these opportunities hopefully can drip down to indigenous groups. In fact, for years the Kuznets hypothesis of economic inequality – the idea that the link between (a) income inequality and (b) income can be represented with an inverted U-curve (market forces first increase and then decrease economic inequality) – has been used to defend the long-term effects of market integration in economic development.[20] Yet, systemic issues further worsen the position of Indigenous peoples as they cannot participate in sectors like manufacturing and services without abandoning their communities or because governments fail to adopt public policies to help those at the bottom of income distribution.[21] Also, Indigenous peoples' capacity to participate in economic activity is severely affected by limited material resources, overt racism, implicit biases, barriers to distribution networks, limits in technical ability and different values, notions of responsibility toward the planet and social and cultural strategies.[22] As explained by James Anaya "[e]ntrenched majority attitudes, social patterns, and legal practices that have been hostile to indigenous cultures for centuries are hard to change."[23] The net result often is the over-empowerment of economic actors

---

[20] Simon Kuznets, *Economic Growth and Income Inequality*, 45 AM. ECON. REV. 1, 1–28 (1955).

[21] Fergus MacKay, *Indigenous Peoples and International Financial Institutions*, in INTERNATIONAL FINANCIAL INSTITUTIONS AND INTERNATIONAL LAW (Daniel D. Bradlow & David B. Hunter eds., 2010).

[22] Karla Hoff & Priyanka Pandey, *Discrimination, Social Identity, and Durable Inequalities*, 96 AM. ECON. REV. 206, 206–211 (2006) (showing that economic incentives are heavily influenced by cultural differences).

[23] S. James Anaya, *International Human Rights and Indigenous Peoples: The Move toward the Multicultural State*, 21 ARIZ. J. INT'L & COMP. 1, 16 (2004).

like MNCs, which are specifically created to succeed in such environments and the relative disempowerment of indigenous groups, who are generally not prepared for it.[24]

Additionally, some treaties require the gradual liberalization of all economic sectors, including that of natural resource extraction.[25] Many of these natural resources are located in indigenous territories and are the only asset for Indigenous peoples to bargain with in negotiations. Again, without adequate protections to empower Indigenous peoples' self-representation, the system is unlikely to improve the bargaining position of indigenous groups vis-à-vis large multinational corporations like oil and gas or mining companies with resources and deep legal, policy and technical expertise and global presence.

Moreover, treaties often establish rights based on nationality. As interested parties must meet the nationality requirements set out in treaties,[26] only foreigners can benefit from the substantive and procedural rights they afford. For instance, trade agreements and investment treaties require states to provide national treatment and most-favored-nation ("MFN") status to foreign entities.[27] Without textual limitations, national treatment obligations (requiring that states provide the same treatment to foreign products, services and investment that is provided to like domestic products, services and investment) effectively disallow a state from giving any economic preference to Indigenous peoples within its own national borders. Furthermore, MFN obligations (requiring that states do not confer benefits to an entity of a third-party state that is more favorable than that which is given to entities of the state that are party to the treaty) make it difficult to enforce any protections for domestic populations such as Indigenous peoples that exist in other economic treaties.[28] Breaches of such obligations give states

---

[24] See, e.g., SUZANA SAWYER, CRUDE CHRONICLES: INDIGENOUS POLITICS, MULTINATIONAL OIL, AND NEOLIBERALISM IN ECUADOR 8 (2004).

[25] The experience under the U.S.–Peru Trade Promotion Agreement, and particularly the annex on tropical hardwoods is illustrative. See Matt Finer et al., *Logging Concessions Enable Illegal Logging Crisis in the Peruvian Amazon*, NATURE, Apr. 17, 2014, https://www.ncbi.nlm.nih.gov/pmc/articles/PMC5380163/.

[26] See Ecuador Bilateral Investment Treaty art. 2, U.S.–Ecuador, Aug. 27, 1993, S. TREATY DOC. No. 103–115 (1997) (requiring states to provide foreign investors treatment that is "no less favorable than that accorded in like situations to investment or associated activities of its own nationals or companies, or of nationals or companies of any third party").

[27] Nicholas DiMascio & Joost Pauwelyn, *Nondiscrimination in Trade and Investment Treaties: Worlds Apart or Two Sides of the Same Coin?*, 102 AM. J. INT'L L. 48, 49–51 (2008).

[28] For example, if state A and state B have an investment treaty in place that contains protections for lands on indigenous territories, such protections could be more difficult to enforce if either state has other investment treaties without such language thanks, in part, to MFN clauses.

and foreign investors the right to sue the infringing state, yet such agreements create no rights for affected local communities or individuals, including Indigenous peoples.

In particular, the policy space to grant special protections can be severely limited by the inclusion of limitations to adopt "performance requirements" – government mandated activities, thresholds or approvals that companies must undertake to trigger investment or trade opportunities, usually connected with exports and use of local content or suppliers.[29] While not always present, these treaty clauses are becoming more and more prevalent in trade and investment agreements.[30] In some limited cases, limitations on subsidization in trade agreements also dissuade governments from adopting similar incentives.[31]

States can and should provide for a level playing field that enables fair economic participation of Indigenous peoples. Rarely states adequately remedy the discrimination resulting from nondiscrimination provisions through domestic policy. As a result, Indigenous peoples rightly feel the need to seek all possible means to protect their interests. In many cases their mobilization efforts have resulted in violence, persecution, prosecutions and death.[32] Sadly, the criminalization of their movement and the imprisonment of their leaders is both a common and an old story, dating back to years prior to

---

[29] See the 2012 U.S. Model Bilateral Investment Treaty, article 8 *Performance Requirements*, visit https://ustr.gov/sites/default/files/BIT%20text%20for%20ACIEP%20Meeting.pdf.

[30] See RUDOLF DOLZER & CHRISTOPH SCHREUER, PRINCIPLES OF INTERNATIONAL INVESTMENT LAW 11 (2nd ed. 2012); Panagiotis Delimatsis & Pierre Sauvé, *Financial Services Trade after the Crisis: Policy and Legal Conjectures*, 13 J. INT'L. ECON. L. 3 837, 850 (2010).

[31] For a discussion on the limitations of the WTO on subsidies, see Teoman M. Hagemeyer, *Tied Aid: Immunization for Export Subsidies Against the Law of the WTO?*, 48 J. WORLD TRADE 259 (2014).

[32] See generally Special Rapporteur on the Rights of Indigenous Peoples, *Report of the Special Rapporteur on the Rights of Indigenous Peoples*, ¶ 39, U.N. Doc. A/HRC/33/42 (Aug. 2016) ("The refusal of the Government of Peru to accept proposals made by Indigenous peoples triggered mobilization, resulting in the tragic deaths of 30 people when the military was deployed in response"); Press Release, Inter-Am. Comm'n H. R., IACHR Condemns the Killing of Berta Cáceres in Honduras (Mar. 4, 2016), https://www.oas.org/en/iachr/media_center/PReleases/2016/024.asp; Human Rights Comm., *Concluding Observations on the Third Periodic Report of Paraguay, Adopted by the Committee at Its 107th Session*, ¶ 15, U.N. Doc. CCPR/C/PRY/CO/3 (Apr. 29, 2013) (stating "[t]he Committee is concerned about the high number of human rights defenders, particularly campesino and indigenous defenders, who have been assaulted, attacked and killed"); Comm. on Econ., Soc. and Cultural Rights, *Concluding Observations on the Initial Report of Indonesia*, ¶ 28, U.N. Doc. E/C.12/IDN/CO/1 (June 19, 2014) (stating in relation to extractive industries that "[i]n many cases, affected communities have not been afforded effective remedies and have, along with human rights defenders working on these cases, been subject to violence and persecution").

the Zapatista movement in Mexico that rose up, in part, against the implementation of NAFTA.[33]

2.3 REREGULATION

FTAs and similar treaties can also indirectly aggravate the problem of extreme poverty and social exclusion by shifting the governance and regulatory priorities of developing states. Often, this looks like prioritizing market efficiency; an increase in trade and investment volumes; and economic growth over poverty alleviation, social mobility, income distribution and democratic empowerment.[34] Undoubtedly, nothing in economic treaties prevent states from prioritizing inclusion, yet – in a setting of public choice dynamics and of limited resources – such a goal can be easily or selectively ignored.

Politically, the right to regulate is a basic and legitimate prerogative of states under international law. However, when states enter into international treaties they voluntarily limit their right to regulate in certain areas or in some fashion in favor of interstate cooperation. Economic treaties, in particular, often have language limiting a state's right to implement legislation or regulation that could negatively impact FDI or the ability of a foreign company or producer to compete fairly against domestic actors.[35] The scope of such constraints may at times be uncertain, particularly considering the open-ended provisions of many legal instruments.[36] As put by Steven Ratner in the context of

---

[33] See Inter-Am. Comm'n H.R, *Criminalization of the Work of Human Rights Defenders*, OEA/ Ser.L/V/II, doc. 49/15 ¶ 49 (Dec. 31, 2015) (stating that "[i]n this regard, the IACHR has received information indicating that in these contexts the criminal justice system is used against indigenous . . . leaders" (footnotes omitted)); Christof Heyns (Special Rapporteur on Extrajudicial, Summary or Arbitrary Executions) *Follow-Up Country Recommendations: Colombia*, ¶ 55, U.N. Doc. A/HRC/20/22/Add.2 (May 15, 2012). In a recent case brought before the Permanent Court of Arbitration, South American Silver Mining is seeking $387 million for the alleged violations of the BIT between the United Kingdom of Great Britain and Northern Ireland by the Plurinational State of Bolivia. The company argued that Bolivia failed to provide full protection and security, based on the "patently unreasonable" decision not to prosecute indigenous leaders protesting the effects of the mining concession. See generally South American Silver Limited (Bermuda) v. The Plurinational State of Bolivia, Case No. 2013–2015, Notice of Arbitration (Perm. Ct. Arb. 2013), https://pcacases.com/web/sendAttach/254.

[34] Dani Rodrik, *Has Globalization Gone Too Far?* 39 Cal. Mgmt. R. 29, 31–32 (1997); see also Dani Rodrik, *Trading in Illusions*, Foreign Policy, Nov. 18, 2009, visit https://foreignpolicy .com/2009/11/18/trading-in-illusions ("By focusing on international integration, governments in poor nations divert human resources, administrative capabilities, and political capital away from more urgent development priorities such as education, public health, industrial capacity, and social cohesion").

[35] DiMascio & Pauwelyn, *supra* note 27.

[36] For a discussion of the constraints in regulatory space, see, Markus Wagner, *Regulatory Space in International Trade Law and International Investment Law*, 36 U. Pa. J. Int'l L. 1 (2014).

investment law, certain provisions do not enhance "an ideal balance between the need for stability and change."[37]

Even in today's world, liberalization and economic interdependence rarely, if ever, demand comprehensive deregulation.[38] However, states may "regulate in the public interest" if they act consistently with their treaty obligations.[39] This often results in what has been called a process of "reregulation" – adopting regulations to facilitate, oversee, and check liberalized markets.[40] This process can be technically complex, as it requires navigating interests, values and legal texts and may chill measures that are effective in realizing some human rights. Some argue, admittedly with limited evidence, that the experience of economic treaties demonstrates that the regulatory function of states and the ability of those states to legislate in the public interest have been put at risk.[41] Particularly, and even more problematic is that governments are dissuaded from adopting laws because of potential liability under an international investor–state dispute settlement or ISDS – the controversial process for reparation used by investors to enforce investment treaties, contracts and foreign investment legislations. This "chilling effect" is felt in various areas and issues, including those concerning Indigenous peoples who are generally excluded from regulatory processes.[42] This phenomenon is exacerbated by the increasing influence of cryptic norms put forth by standard-setting organizations.[43] As for the WTO, Gregory Shaffer concludes that the institution's focus on regulation that is "least trade restrictive" influences decisions made by domestic lawmakers and has important

---

[37] Steven Ratner, *International Investment Law through the Lens of Global Justice*, 20 J. INT'L ECON. L. 747, 764 (2017).

[38] DAVID BEETHAM, UNELECTED OLIGARCHY 5 (2011).

[39] See Megan Davis, *To Bind or Not to Bind: The United Nations Declaration on the Rights of Indigenous Peoples Five Years On*, 19 AUSTL. INT'L L.J. 17, 29 (2012) (noting that on balancing indigenous rights is set "any conflict is usually resolved in favour of the non-Indigenous public interest").

[40] Gregory Shaffer, *How the WTO Shapes Regulatory Governance*, 9 REG. & GOVERNANCE 1, 3 (2015).

[41] See U.N. Office of the High Commissioner, *UN Experts Voice Concern over Adverse Impact of Free Trade and Investment Agreements on Human Rights*, June 2, 2015, http://www.ohchr.org/EN/NewsEvents/Pages/DisplayNews.aspx?NewsID=16031.

[42] See Alfred de Zayas (Independent Expert on the Promotion of a Democratic and Equitable International Order), *Report of the Independent Expert on the Promotion of a Democratic and Equitable International Order*, ¶ 11, U.N. Doc. A/HRC/33/40 (July 12, 2016) (stating "[t]he regulatory chill caused by the mere existence of investor-State dispute settlements has effectively dissuaded many States from adopting much-needed health and environmental protection measures").

[43] Lawrence L. Herman, *The New Multilateralism: The Shift to Private Global Regulation*, C.D. HOWE INST., Aug. 4–5, 2012, visit https://www.cdhowe.org/sites/default/files/attachments/research_papers/mixed/Commentary_360_0.pdf.

distributional effects.[44] Hence, international economic agreements constrain policy or regulatory space, and, in some instances, influence the state's decision whether to protect the basic human rights of its inhabitants.[45]

2.4 INEQUALITY

Too often, poverty is "characterized by a vicious cycle of powerlessness, stigmatization, discrimination, exclusion and material deprivation."[46] The combined effects of the vicious cycle that comprises powerlessness to influence the law; that facilitates discrimination (or its effects); and that results in the exclusion from governance priorities is unlikely to end the material deficit suffered by Indigenous peoples. On the contrary, this cycle is likely to entrench the economic effects of an unequal system where economically powerful and politically influential actors make decisions that affect those already disenfranchised.[47] Accordingly, this cycle is the textbook example of the conditions that exacerbate inequality.

For many indigenous groups the likely result of the main instruments that enable interdependence is the increase in inequality. Despite the aggregate economic benefits that countries enjoy, empirical evidence indicates that Indigenous peoples are not proportionally better off.[48] For instance, Latin America enjoyed a "golden decade" from 2000 to 2010, but the benefits therefrom were unevenly distributed. The disparities in poverty and extreme poverty were, respectively, 2.7 times and 3.0 times higher among Indigenous

---

[44] Shaffer, *supra* note 40, at 17.

[45] Emilie Hafner-Burton, Forced to Be Good: Why Trade Agreements Boost Human Rights, 4 (2009).

[46] Magdalena Sepúlveda Carmona (Special Rapporteur on Extreme Poverty and Human Rights), *Report of the Special Rapporteur on Extreme Poverty and Human Rights*, ¶ 12, U.N. Doc. A/HRC/23/36, 11 (Mar. 11, 2013).

[47] *See generally* Comm'n on Human Rights, *Discrimination Against Indigenous Peoples: Transnational Investments and Operations on the Lands of Indigenous Peoples*, U.N. Doc. E/CN.4/Sub.2/1994/40 (June 15, 1994) (detailing impacts of corporations on indigenous peoples in Asia and Africa).

[48] World Bank Group, Indigenous Latin America in the Twenty-First Century: The First Decade 15 (2015), https://openknowledge.worldbank.org/bitstream/handle/10986/23751/IndigenousoLatoyoootheofirstodecade.pdf?sequence=1&isAllowed=y ("[T]he results of the first decade of the twenty-first century – considered by many the golden decade of economic growth for Latin America – have been mixed for indigenous Latin Americans. While important steps have been taken to raise awareness on the special needs and rights of Indigenous peoples, most countries and development agencies still lack institutionalized and efficient mechanisms to implement Indigenous peoples' rights"). Cf. Ricardo A. Godoy et al. *Do Markets Worsen Economic Inequality? Kuznets in the Bush*, 32 Human Ecology, 339–64 (2004).

households in comparison to nonindigenous households.[49] On average, an indigenous person makes a third of the income made by a nonindigenous person and possesses less than a tenth of the wealth.[50]

Indigenous peoples are often impacted in other ways that ultimately increase inequality. For instance, they may be dispossessed of their lands or have them encroached upon by concessions for resource extraction, development projects or even the creation of protected areas for environmental conservation. International and national courts have found that these instances may violate substantive rights and lack procedural guarantees, remediation and compensation,[51] yet in most cases no reparations are provided, much less any enjoyment of the benefits of the development initiative or projects.[52] Such loss of control over the use of lands without effective compensation and economic alternatives inevitably leads to lower economic capacity, less social mobility and greater inequality.

* * *

---

[49] World Bank Group, *supra* note 48, at 59; see also, Bello, *The Great Deceleration*, Economist, Nov. 20, 2014, visit https://www.economist.com/the-americas/2014/11/20/ the-great-deceleration ("It was great while it lasted. In a golden period from 2003 to 2010 Latin America's economies grew at an annual average rate of close to 5%, wages rose and unemployment fell, more than 50m people were lifted out of poverty and the middle class swelled to more than a third of the population. But now the growth spurt is over . . . Latin America is decelerating faster than much of the rest of the emerging world").

[50] See generally, Andy Sumner, *The New Face of Poverty: How Has the Composition of Poverty in Low Income and Lower Middle-Income Countries (Excluding China) Changed since the 1990s?*, Inst. of Dev. Studies, Working Paper No. 408, 2012), http://www.ids.ac.uk/files/dmfile/ Wp408.pdf; Save the Children, Born Equal: How Reducing Inequality Could Give Our Children a Better Future (2012), https://www.savethechildren.org.uk/content/dam/ global/reports/advocacy/born-equal.pdf; Earth Matters: Indigenous Peoples, the Extractive Industries and Corporate Social Responsibility (Ciaran O'Faircheallaigh & Saleem Ali eds., 2017).

[51] See Case of the Saramaka People v. Suriname, Preliminary Objections, Merits, Reparations, and Costs, Judgment, Inter-Am. Ct. H.R. (ser. C) No. 172, ¶ 127 (Nov. 28, 2007) (stating "the Court has previously held that . . . a State may restrict the use and enjoyment of the right to property where the restrictions are: a) previously established by law; b) necessary; c) proportional, and d) with the aim of achieving a legitimate objective in a democratic society").

[52] *Id.* ¶¶ 138–39 (stating that "[t]he second safeguard the State must ensure when considering development or investment plans within Saramaka territory is that of reasonably sharing the benefits of the project with the Saramaka people. The concept of benefit-sharing . . . can be found in various international instruments regarding indigenous and tribal peoples' rights") James Anaya (Special Rapporteur on the Rights of Indigenous Peoples), *Extractive Industries Operating Within or Near Indigenous Territories*, ¶¶ 30–55, U.N. Doc. A/HRC/18/35 (July 11, 2011) (summarizing the negative effects of extractive operations globally).

International economic law fosters rules, policies and principles that support private actors while dissuading states from exercising certain sovereign powers. As a result, groups with the least agency, like Indigenous peoples, may end up relatively worse off *if/when* international economic law ignores these effects.[53] Before elaborating on how to address these imbalances, the next chapter reviews some of the main protections for Indigenous peoples currently available under international economic law, both in theory and in practice.

---

[53] See Olivier De Schutter (Special Rapporteur on the Right to Food), *Mission to Malaysia*, ¶¶ 64–5, U.N. Doc. A/HRC/25/57/Add.2 (Feb. 3, 2014) (highlighting "problems faced in their access to traditional sources of livelihood as a result of encroachment on their lands and the degradation of ecosystems caused by development projects, logging and the expansion of palm oil plantations"); Rita Izsak (Independent Expert on Minority Issues), *Mission to Cameroon* (*Sept. 2–11 2013*), ¶ 37, U.N. Doc. A/HRC/25/56/Add.1 (Jan. 31, 2014) (stating "many Pygmy communities have been displaced by major projects, including a deep-sea port, gas plants, the Chad-Cameroon oil pipeline, and forestry and logging projects. Palm and rubber plantations have also displaced the Bagyeli, and their former forest habitats have become 'no-go' areas for them. They rarely receive compensation for their land, jobs, health care or other benefits").

3

Indigenous Peoples under International Economic Law

For decades we have seen an increase in the number and in the development of frameworks that encourage economic globalization. We have also observed a similar path in the expansion of the international law frameworks that protect human rights, including indigenous human rights. These parallel developments have resulted in separate, almost independent fields; this despite the fact that both fields – international economic and human rights law – are fundamental to public international law after World War II (WWII).

At least two reasons might explain why historically there has not been a strong connection between human rights law and international economic law, especially international trade and investment law.[1] While international trade and FDI regulation have developed through the General Agreement on Tariffs and Trade ("GATT"), the WTO, free trade agreements ("FTAs") and bilateral investment treaties ("BITs"), human rights institutions have evolved around the UN and, more recently, regional systems.[2] The result is, in Robert Wai's words, that "each field utilize[s] distinct discourses and frameworks for addressing similar problems."[3] In particular, human rights frameworks use a discourse of universal values, self-determination and accountability, whereas international economic

---

[1]   Robert Wai, *Countering, Branding, Dealing: Using Economic and Social Rights in and around the International Trade Regime,* 14 EUR. J. INT'L. L. 35, 45 (2003).
[2]   For a discussion on trade and investment regimes, see Sergio Puig, *The Merging of International Trade and Investment Law,* 33 BERKELEY J. INT'L L. 1, 39 (2015). For human rights, see Philip Alston, *Does the Past Matter? On the Origins of Human Rights,* 126 HARV. L. REV. 2043 (2013) (reviewing JENNY S. MARTINEZ, THE SLAVE TRADE AND THE ORIGINS OF INTERNATIONAL HUMAN RIGHTS LAW (2012)).
[3]   Wai, *supra* note 1, at 43.

law uses a language of reciprocity and restraint, nondiscrimination, self-interest and joint gains.[4]

Nonetheless, officials and scholars have recognized the parallel goals toward which both international economic law and human rights law strive. Efforts have also been made to address the link between the business activities promoted by international economic law and human rights. Chief among these efforts is the UN Human Rights Council's Guiding Principles on Business and Human Rights.[5] The Guiding Principles reiterate the human rights duties that apply to all states, international organizations and business enterprises, "regardless of their size, sector, location, ownership and structure."[6] The Guiding Principles reflect the general effort to understand how states, as well as non-state actors, are implicated when commercial activities conflict with human rights. Partly because of this effort, many large corporations have taken active steps to prevent violations through the adoption of and compliance with corporate social responsibility ("CSR") policies.[7]

Beyond any doubt, states, international organizations, and private businesses have distinct but complementary duties concerning human rights. States are obligated to respect, protect, and fulfill human rights within their jurisdiction. International organizations are obligated to ensure that their activities, like financing infrastructure or peacekeeping in conflict zones, conform with (and in some cases protect) human rights.[8] Business actors

---

4   For human rights, see, e.g., International Covenant on Civil and Political Rights, 1966 (CCPR), art. 1(1); International Covenant on Economic, Social and Cultural Rights, 1966 (CESCR), art. 1(1).

5   U.N. Human Rights Council, *Guiding Principles on Business and Human Rights*, U.N. Doc. HR/PUB/11/04, at 1 (June 16, 2011).

6   *Id.* at 15. Other international organizations incorporated aspects of the U.N. Guiding Principles. For example, the Organization for Economic Co-operation and Development ("OECD") revised its Guidelines for Multinational Enterprises. OECD, *Annual Report on the OECD Guidelines for Multinational Enterprises* (2017), http://mneguidelines.oecd.org/2017-Annual-Report-MNE-Guidelines-EN.pdf; see also *Business and Human Rights*, U.N. HUMAN RIGHTS OFF. OF THE HIGH COMM'R, http://www.ohchr.org/EN/Issues/Business/Pages/BusinessIndex.aspx.

7   See, e.g., *Accountable and Inclusive Governance*, NESTLE, visit http://www.nestle.com/csv/what-is-csv/governance; *Addressing Human Rights Impacts*, NESTLE, visit http://www.nestle.com/csv/communities/human-rights-impacts; *Our Approach to Human and Workplace Rights*, COCA-COLA, visit http://www.coca-colacompany.com/our-company/human-workplace-rights; *PepsiCo*, BUS. & HUM. RTS. RESOURCE CTR., visit https://business-humanrights.org/en/pepsico-0.

8   See Nuhanović v. Netherlands, Case No. LJN:BR5388, Judgment, ¶¶ 5.8, 5.9, (July 5, 2011), http://opil.ouplaw.com/view/10.1093/law:ildc/1742nl11.case.1/law-ildc-1742nl11; Int'l Law Comm'n, Rep. of the Sixty-Third Session, Draft Articles on the Responsibility of International Organizations with Commentaries, U.N. Doc. A/66/10, at 52 (2011); Andrew Clapham, Human

do not have the same responsibility as states or international organizations. However, due to the increase in international mechanisms of accountability, it is becoming very much in their interest to, at the very least, respect this body of law.[9] Moreover, in most states, human rights are protected under domestic law (including often under a constitution), and a business implicated in the violation of human rights might be subject to civil, criminal or other proceedings under that body of law. Some states extend these obligations further. In India, for instance, the 2013 Companies Act, uniquely, requires companies incorporated under the laws of the country to implement CSR policy.[10]

The responsibility imposed on state and non-state actors to follow human rights norms when carrying out official and business activities is best developed in the Guiding Principles, or the "Protect, Respect and Remedy" Framework. The framework calls on both states and businesses in laying its foundation on the following three pillars:

(a) States' existing obligations to respect, protect and fulfill human rights and fundamental freedoms;
(b) The role of business enterprises as specialized organs of society performing specialized functions, required to comply with all applicable laws and to respect human rights;
(c) The need for rights and obligations to be matched to appropriate and effective remedies when breached.[11]

Thus, the framework confirms that states are the primary duty-bearers, but private actors such as business enterprises are not insulated from the demands of international human rights law. In this way, international law complements

Rights Obligations of Non-state Actors 142–43 (2006); see also, e.g., Roberto Danino, *Legal Opinion on Human Rights and the Work of the World Bank* 17, Jan. 27, 2006, visit http://opil .ouplaw.com/view/10.1093/law-oxio/e215.013.1/law-oxio-e215-regGroup-1-law-oxio-e215-source .pdf.

[9] The new United States-Mexico-Canada Agreement (USMCA), addresses the issue of Corporate Social Responsibility (CSR). *See* United States-Mexico-Canada Agreement (USCMA), Can.-Mex.-U.S., Chapter 14, art. 14.17, *opened for signature* Sept. 30, 2018. However, the Parties only reaffirm the importance of each Party encouraging enterprises operating within its territory or subject to its jurisdiction to incorporate voluntarily into their internal policies internationally recognized standards, guidelines and principles of CSR that address areas such as labor, environment, gender equality, human rights, indigenous and aboriginal peoples' rights and corruption.

[10] Afra Afsharipour & Shruti Rana, *The Emergence of New Corporate Social Responsibility Regimes in China and India*, 14 UC Davis Bus. L.J. 175, 217–18 (2014).

[11] U.N. Human Rights Council, *supra* note 5, at 1.

the state's prerogative to regulate business activities.[12] Notably, the Guiding Principles explicitly focus on avoiding adverse impacts on human rights by economic actors. The emerging field of business and human rights offers limited, but much needed, conceptual clarity for linking human rights law and its norms with states and non-state businesses and their activities. Nevertheless, international economic law and human rights law continue to attract practical and academic treatment as two almost unrelated fields.

Now, human rights law includes protections that apply exclusively to Indigenous peoples. In other words, within the field of international human rights law, international indigenous human rights are specific rules and norms that protect and empower Indigenous peoples, who face particular challenges. Before addressing the question on how international economic law and indigenous rights interact, first I briefly describe the broad contours and many of the sources of the international human rights regime as it concerns Indigenous peoples.

3.1 GENERAL PROTECTIONS UNDER INTERNATIONAL LAW

As complementary to the rights that international law recognizes for individuals as humans, international law also recognizes collective rights of indigenous groups.[13] While Indigenous peoples' rights (or some of these rights) have been associated with minority rights, indigenous rights' advocates have frequently rejected calling indigenous groups "minorities" in their attempts to establish a separate regime with greater legal entitlements and distinct from minority rights – a distinction with a long and important pedigree.[14] However, no authoritative definition of "Indigenous peoples" exists. Rather, a series of factors are considered relevant for determining who is indigenous.[15] Among

---

[12] For a comprehensive treatment of the topic, see Steven R. Ratner, *Corporations and Human Rights: A Theory of Legal Responsibility*, 111 YALE L.J. 443, 466–67 (2001).

[13] International economic treaties have contributed to the collective rights recognition. For example, some FTAs protect collective rights of Indigenous peoples such as intellectual property rights. See Section 3.2.1.

[14] S. James Anaya, Indigenous Peoples in International Law, 2nd ed., 3–4 (2004).

[15] For a discussion of the emergence and conceptual complexities of the field, see Benedict Kingsbury, *"Indigenous Peoples" in International Law: A Constructivist Approach to the Asian Controversy*, 92 AM. J. INT'L. L. 414, 419–20 (1998); see also Erica-Irene A. Daes (Chairperson-Rapporteur on the Concept of "Indigenous People"), *Standard-Setting Activities: Evolution of Standards concerning the Rights of Indigenous People*, ¶ 69, U.N. Doc. E/CN.4/Sub.2/AC.4/1996/2 (June 10, 1996) (stating "the factors which modern international organizations and legal experts ... have considered relevant to the understanding of the concept of 'indigenous' include: (a) Priority in time, with respect to the occupation and use of a specific territory; (b) The voluntary perpetuation of cultural distinctiveness, which may include aspects of language, social

these, the "experience of subjugation, marginalization, dispossession, exclusion or discrimination" is key.[16] These elements are rooted in economic, social and political considerations, and have justified the development of rights owed to Indigenous peoples as a protected category or class – a group of people with common characteristics whose interests are legally protected.[17]

Today, few, if any, dispute the need for the recognition of such protections – although controversy exists around the exact rights, context of application and the content of such protections. The exceptional treatment is needed for many empirical and policy reasons. For one, despite the fact that Indigenous peoples make up only 5 percent of the world's population, they represent 15 percent of the world's poor.[18] More dramatically, some estimate that Indigenous peoples represent one-third of the world's one billion extremely poor rural people.[19] These numbers are rather vexing and speak volumes to the problem and systematic exclusion, especially considering that Indigenous peoples' traditional territories often coincide with the world's most biologically diverse areas and are rich in natural, mineral and other resources.[20] Today, such lands comprise 80 percent of the Earth's remaining healthy ecosystems.[21]

---

organization, religion and spiritual values, modes of production, laws and institutions; (c) Self-identification, as well as recognition by other groups, or by State authorities, as a distinct collectivity; and (d) an experience of subjugation, marginalization, dispossession, exclusion or discrimination, whether or not these conditions persist").

[16] Anaya *supra* note 14, at 3–4. See also Human Rights Council *Report of the Special Rapporteur on the Rights of Indigenous Peoples*, thirty-third session, A/HRC/33/42 (August 11, 2016) ¶15, visit https://www.ohchr.org/Documents/Issues/IPeoples/SR/A_HRC_33_42_en.docx.

[17] A strand of literature in the law and development field has focused on human rights and Indigenous peoples. See, e.g., James Thuo Gathii, *Imperialism, Colonialism, and International Law*, 54 Buff. L. Rev. 1013, 1043 (2007) (discussing the relationship between English common law and international law and its effects on the decolonization of British protectorates); see also, J. Oloka-Onyango, *Reinforcing Marginalized Rights in an Age of Globalization: International Mechanisms, Non-state Actors, and the Struggle for Peoples' Rights in Africa*, 18 Am. U. Int'l L. Rev. 851, 866–67 (2003) (examining the case of the Ogoni peoples of Nigeria).

[18] United Nations Department of Economic and Social Affairs, State of the World's Indigenous Peoples (New York: United Nations, 2009), at 21.

[19] World Bank, *Decline of Global Extreme Poverty Continues but Has Slowed*, Sept. 19, 2018, visit http://www.worldbank.org/en/news/press-release/2018/09/19/decline-of-global-extreme-poverty-continues-but-has-slowed-world-bank (defining extremely poor people as those who live on less than US$1.90 per day).

[20] Claudia Sobrevila, The Role of Indigenous Peoples in Biodiversity Conservation: The Natural but Often Forgotten Partners, at xii (2008).

[21] Glob. Envtl. Facility, Indigenous Communities and Biodiversity 9 (2008), https://www.thegef.org/sites/default/files/publications/indigenous-community-biodiversity_0.pdf.

Historically, Indigenous peoples' struggles relate to the denial of recognition of autonomy and self-determination, the protection of their culture and territories and the property and resources therein.[22] While Indigenous peoples have won a few important victories in recent years, such victories were not won easily. For instance, it took twenty years of international advocacy and negotiation until the UN General Assembly adopted the Declaration on the Rights of Indigenous Peoples or UNDRIP, now more than a decade old.[23] The UNDRIP is perhaps the most important instrument that enunciates the core rights due to Indigenous peoples. It explicitly sets out the right of self-determination as a means for the protection, promotion and development of society, culture and economy for indigenous groups. In Article 3, it states: "Indigenous peoples have the right of self-determination. By virtue of that right they freely determine their political status and freely pursue their economic, social and cultural development." Other provisions protect the right to "manifest, practice, develop and teach their spiritual and religious traditions, customs and ceremonies."[24] Articles 21, 23 and 31 state a right of Indigenous peoples to develop politically, economically and socially, including setting their own priorities for development. Fundamentally, Article 26 expands on this idea, which is core to a proper understanding of the interaction of indigenous rights with international economic law:

(1) Indigenous peoples have the right to the lands, territories and resources that they have traditionally owned, occupied or otherwise used or acquired.

(2) Indigenous peoples have the right to own, use, develop and control the lands, territories and resources that they possess by reason of traditional ownership or other traditional occupation or use, as well as those that they have otherwise acquired.

(3) States shall give legal recognition and protection to these lands, territories and resources. Such recognition shall be conducted with due respect to

---

[22] James (Sa'ke'j) Youngblood Henderson, Indigenous Diplomacy and the Rights of Peoples: Achieving UN Recognition 11 (2008).

[23] G.A. Res. 61/295, annex, Declaration on the Rights of Indigenous Peoples (Sept. 13, 2007) [hereinafter UNDRIP]. Indigenous rights are protected by different sources, see, Int'l Law Ass'n, The Hague Conference: Rights of Indigenous Peoples 51 (2010) (stating it is "indisputable that indigenous peoples are of concern to customary international law").

[24] UNDRIP, art. 12

the customs, traditions and land tenure systems of the indigenous peoples concerned.[25]

The American Declaration on the Rights of Indigenous Peoples also reflects the recognition of indigenous protections.[26] Additionally, minimum standards of indigenous rights are made explicit in the International Labor Organization (Convention No. 169) on Indigenous and Tribal Peoples. And, in the field of business and human rights, the UN Guidelines recommend particular attention to specific groups and populations, including Indigenous peoples.[27]

It would be impossible to do justice to a complex field of law in just a few pages. Instead, I refer to some of the most important works and make some important summary remarks. Though indigenous rights and minority rights have much in common, analytically, under international law, indigenous rights are derived from a very distinct type of legal obligation.[28] While there is academic disagreement as to the extent and reach of these protections, the recognition of indigenous rights (and its distinctiveness) is well established.[29]

---

[25] *Id.*, art. 26

[26] Organization of American States, American Declaration on the Rights of Indigenous Peoples, June 14, 2016, AG/RES 2888 (XLVI-O/16); see also U.N. Development Programme, Social and Environmental Standards, at 36–41 (June 2014), http://www.undp.org/content/dam/undp/library/corporate/Social-and-Environmental-Policies-and-Procedures/UNDPs-Social-and-Environmental-Standards-ENGLISH.pdf; Int'l Fund for Agricultural Dev., *IFAD Policy on Engagement with Indigenous Peoples*, U.N. Doc. EB 2009/97/R.3 (Sept. 14, 2009), https://www.ifad.org/documents/38711624/39417924/ip_policy_e.pdf/a7cd3bc3–8622-4302-afdf-6db216ad5feb; Global Envtl. Facility, *GEF Policy on Agency Minimum Standards on Environmental and Social Safeguards*, at 24, U.N. Doc. GEF/C.41/10/Rev.1 (Nov. 18, 2011), https://www.thegef.org/sites/default/files/council-meeting-documents/C.41.10.Rev_1.Policy_on_Environmental_and_Social_Safeguards.Final%20of%20Nov%202018.pdf; U.N. Food and Agriculture Org., *FAO Policy on Indigenous and Tribal Peoples* (2010), http://www.fao.org/fileadmin/user_upload/newsroom/docs/FAO_policy.pdf; *Guidelines on Free, Prior and Informed Consent*, UN-REDD (Jan. 2013), https://www.unclearn.org/sites/default/files/inventory/un-reddo5.pdf. Among the International Financial Institutions, see *Environmental and Social Framework*, WORLD BANK, https://www.worldbank.org/en/projects-operations/environmental-and-social-framework.

[27] U.N. Human Rights Council, *supra* note 5, at 1.

[28] ANAYA, *supra* note 14, at 134 ("International practice has ... tended to treat indigenous peoples and minorities as comprising distinct but overlapping categories subject to common normative considerations").

[29] Indigenous people may rely on minority rights if their role as a minority is also accepted. However, even if minority rights are relied upon, such rights may fail to address issues central to Indigenous peoples, such as self-determination, land use and governance. See Douglas Sanders, *Collective Rights*, 13 HUM. RTS. Q. 368, 376 (1991).

What makes indigenous rights different is that they are recognized because of a political or economic status, often connected with the conditions of historically subjugated communities that have been dispossessed, brutalized and discriminated against.[30] Hence, the normative goals of indigenous rights include political empowerment and autonomy (by means of rights to participation and self-determination to pursue their own priorities for economic, social and cultural development) and expansion of economic opportunity and participation (by means of rights to property, culture and nondiscrimination in relation to lands, territories and natural resources), among other laudable goals.[31] As James Anaya puts it:

> The contemporary human rights regime concerning indigenous peoples advances, on the one hand, cultural integrity and autonomy and, on the other, participatory engagement. This dual thrust reflects the view that indigenous peoples are entitled to be different but are not necessarily to be considered *a priori* unconnected from larger social and political structures. Rather, indigenous groups – whether characterized as communities, peoples, nations, or other – are appropriately viewed as simultaneously distinct from, yet part of, larger units of social and political interaction, units that may include indigenous federations, the states within which they live and the global community itself.[32]

---

[30] *See* George K. Foster, *Foreign Investment and Indigenous Peoples: Options for Promoting Equilibrium Between Economic Development and Indigenous Rights*, 33 MICH. J. INT'L L. 627, 669 (2012). ("[E]ven if a country enacts new laws … there is no reason to expect that the enforcement of those new laws … will be any more effective or consistent than that of preexisting indigenous-rights laws.").

[31] S. James Anaya, *Indigenous Peoples' Participatory Rights in Relation to Decisions about Natural Resource Extraction: The More Fundamental Issue of What Rights Indigenous Peoples Have in Lands and Resources*, 22 ARIZ. J. INTL. COMP. L. 7, 7 (2005) ("In asserting property rights, indigenous peoples seek protection of economic, jurisdictional, and cultural interests, all of which are necessary for them to pursue their economic, social, and cultural development"). For a discussion of the historical underpinnings of the struggle of indigenous peoples for self-determination in North America, see Robert A. Williams, Jr., *Columbus's Legacy: Law As an Instrument of Racial Discrimination against Indigenous Peoples' Rights of Self-Determination*, 8 ARIZ. J. INTL. COMP. L. 51, 52 (1991) ("The cultural racism of Europeans … denied the idea that indigenous tribal peoples should be in control of their own destinies, and imposed upon them instead a legal regime of alien domination that refused recognition of their fundamental human rights of self-determination").

[32] *Id.* Anaya, at 60.

3.2 SPECIFIC PROTECTIONS IN ECONOMIC REGIMES

The rise of global trade, foreign investment and international finance correlates with an increase in preferential trade agreements,[33] bilateral investment treaties,[34] financing by development banks and agencies[35] and treaties containing intellectual property (or IP) provisions.[36] Recently, Indigenous peoples, their governments and advocacy groups have sought concrete protections against the potentially negative effects of these instruments within these agreements and, through various fora, have defended a more beneficial articulation of the relationship between the two fields of law. As explained shortly, these efforts have been only moderately successful.

In this next section, I describe the provisions and analyze the relative strength of existing measures to protect Indigenous peoples in economic regimes. I divide the section into four subsections, one for each of the main pillars of the field of international economic law: IP, finance, trade and investment (in that order). As I explain here, there is a rigorous debate as to the efficacy of the measures in place, the appropriateness of the substance and legal form of such protections and what constitutes the best way forward.

3.2.1 *Intellectual Property*

The debate within the field of international IP focuses on the threats Indigenous peoples face from theft and appropriation of, and lack of fair

---

[33] *Regional Trade Agreements: Facts and Figures*, WORLD TRADE ORG., https://www.wto.org/english/tratop_e/region_e/regfac_e.htm (noting that between 1948 and 1994, 125 regional trade agreements were sent to the GATT, whereas since 1995, "over 400 additional arrangements" have been sent).

[34] U.N. Conf. on Trade & Dev., *International Investment Agreements Navigator*, INV. POL'Y HUB, http://investmentpolicyhub.unctad.org/IIA (showing that as of October 2018 there was a total of 2,953 bilateral investment treaties, with 2,358 in force).

[35] Rebecca M. Nelson, *Multilateral Development Banks: Overview and Issues for Congress*, 5 CONG. RES. SERV. (2015), https://digital.library.unt.edu/ark:/67531/metadc795908/m1/1/high_res_d/R41170_2015Dec02.pdf (showing an increase in lending by multilateral development banks from 2000 to 2015).

[36] Christine Haight Farley, *Trips-Plus Trade and Investment Agreements: Why More May Be Less for Economic Development*, 35 U. PA. J. INT'L. L. 1061, 1061 (2014) (noting the rise of intellectual property provisions within free trade agreements and bilateral investment treaties).

compensation for, traditional knowledge,[37] genetic and biological resources[38] and intangible cultural heritage and folklore.[39]

Next, I elaborate on the debates of these specific regimes. As I explain, such debates are nuanced and in some areas less ideological than in others.[40] For one, traditional knowledge has historically been treated as within the public domain – hence freely available "for exploitation by third parties."[41] Without additional protections, third parties would rarely seek the consent of indigenous communities before use of traditional knowledge; even less, to share with indigenous communities the economic benefits stemming from the exclusivity protections and use.[42] In the cases of biotechnology products, there is an additional concern that this practice could also deprive indigenous groups of the use of traditional medical remedies without having to pay royalties – a practice referred to as bio-piracy.[43]

---

[37] The appropriate definition of the term "traditional knowledge" has generated significant debate. The World International Property Organization ("WIPO") defines traditional knowledge as "knowledge, know-how, skills and practices that are developed, sustained and passed on from generation to generation within a community, often forming part of its cultural or spiritual identity." *Traditional Knowledge*, WORLD INTELL. PROP. ORG., visit http://www.wipo.int/tk/en/tk. Ikechi Mgbeoji argues that traditional knowledge encompasses "a diverse range of tradition-based innovations and creations arising from intellectual activity in the industrial, literary, or artistic fields of indigenous and traditional peoples"; IKECHI MGBEOJI, GLOBAL BIOPIRACY: PATENTS, PLANTS, AND INDIGENOUS KNOWLEDGE 9 (2006). However, some scholars disagree with the use of the word "traditional" as it potentially evokes colonial-era imagery and prefer the term "indigenous knowledge." Fikret Berkes, Johan Colding & Carl Folke, *Rediscovery of Traditional Ecological Knowledge As Adaptive Management*, 10 ECOLOGICAL APPLICATIONS 1251 (2000).

[38] According to WIPO, "[g]enetic resources (GRs) refer to genetic material of actual or potential value. Genetic material is any material of plant, animal, microbial or other origin containing functional units of heredity"; *Genetic Resources*, WORLD INTELL. PROP. ORG., visit http://www.wipo.int/tk/en/genetic.

[39] According to WIPO, folklore (also referred to as "traditional cultural expressions") "may include music, dance, art, designs, names, signs and symbols, performances, ceremonies, architectural forms, handicrafts and narratives, or many other artistic or cultural expressions." *Traditional Cultural Expressions*, WORLD INTELL. PROP. ORG., visit http://www.wipo.int/tk/en/folklore.

[40] Ravi Soopramanien, *International Trade in Indigenous Cultural Heritage: What Protection Does International Law Provide for Indigenous Cultural Goods and Services in International Commerce?* 53 STAN. J. INT'L. L. 225, 227 (2017) (describing these positions as a way for "indigenous peoples to assert their right to increased economic independence vis-à-vis their host states").

[41] Laurence R. Helfer, *Toward a Human Rights Framework for Intellectual Property*, 40 UC DAVIS L. REV. 971, 982–83 (2007).

[42] See *id.* at 980–91.

[43] MGBEOJI, *supra* note 37, at 12 (bio-piracy is used to describe "a misappropriation of indigenous peoples['] knowledge and biocultural resources, especially through the use of intellectual

Indigenous cultural expressions are also inadequately protected under IP frameworks.[44] Indigenous communities can register symbols and other expressions under national IP processes. However, these protections tend to be burdensome and partial, and often exclude intangible practices (such as sacred ceremonies or dances) and slightly modified copies, often considered in the "public domain."[45]

To a large degree, these debates reflect the tension between indigenous and "Western" notions of property rights, individual and collective ownership and differentiation and commoditization of knowledge.[46] The tensions raise many issues of the legitimacy and equity of forms of recognition, appropriation, use and legal classification of indigenous knowledge and practices. Very often, at the core of these tensions are two fundamental paradigms of international law: On the one hand, relativism – premised on the overarching character of sovereignty – and on the other, universalism – based on the belief of shared human values.[47] The tension is often perceived as so extreme that some argue international IP is inherently in conflict with indigenous interests.[48] As I now explain, these competing views have led to modest protection of Indigenous peoples within different frameworks. More importantly, while modest, imperfect and evolving some areas of IP like traditional knowledge are notorious for the "widening recognition of the significance and value of Indigenous" diversity and distinct value systems.[49]

---

property mechanisms"); Matthew L. M. Fletcher, *Theoretical Restrictions on the Sharing of Indigenous Biological Knowledge: Implications for Freedom of Speech in Tribal Law*, 14 KAN. J.L. & PUB. POL'Y 525, 528–29 (2005) (documenting two examples of the bio-piracy of indigenous biological knowledge in North America and discussing the exploitation of indigenous biological knowledge generally); Ian Vincent McGonigle, *Patenting Nature or Protecting Culture? Ethnopharmacology and Indigenous Intellectual Property Rights*, 3 J.L. & BIOSCIENCES 217, 220 (2016) (describing the patenting of a genetically modified version of the Hawaiian plant Taro).

[44] Srividhya Ragavan, *Protection of Traditional Knowledge*, 2 MINN. INTELL. PROP. REV. 1, 14–17 (2001).

[45] Angela R. Riley, *"Straight Stealing": Towards an Indigenous System of Cultural Property Protection*, 80 WASH. L. REV. 69, 79–81 (2005).

[46] See Mauro Barelli, *The United Nations Declaration on the Rights of Indigenous Peoples: A Human Rights Framework for Intellectual Property Rights*, in INDIGENOUS INTELLECTUAL PROPERTY: A HANDBOOK OF CONTEMPORARY RESEARCH 47, 56 (Matthew Rimmer ed., 2015).

[47] See Jack Donnelly, *Cultural Relativism and Universal Human Rights*, 6 HUM. RTS. Q. 400, 400–19 (1984).

[48] Preston Hardison & Kelly Bannister, *Ethics in Ethnobiology: History, International Law and Policy, and Contemporary Issues*, in ETHNOBIOLOGY 27, 41 (E. N. Anderson et al. eds., 2011).

[49] For an excellent treatment of the topic, see Anthony Taubman, *New Dialogues, New Pathways: Reframing the Debate on Intellectual Property and Traditional Knowledge*, 58 WASHBURN L.J., 373–97 (2019).

Traditional Knowledge: The World Intellectual Property Organization ("WIPO") is a specialized agency of the UN tasked with promoting balanced IP protections worldwide.[50] Due to the increasing visibility of arguments against misappropriation and misuse of indigenous resources, WIPO has "become increasingly involved in norm-setting in the[se] areas."[51] This involvement suggests the express political linkage by states between harmonization of IP law formalities and the social and legal contexts of Indigenous peoples.

As for issues of traditional knowledge, WIPO has pursued two important objectives: to establish defensive protections against its misuse and to encourage positive protections in the form of remedies to protect the unfair exploitation of indigenous knowledge.[52] In this context, WIPO also oversees indigenous knowledge issues through discussions held by an intergovernmental committee.[53] A direct effect of the work of the committee has been effecting change in other economic international organizations, including the WTO to address issues pertinent to traditional knowledge under the IP (i.e., patent) provisions.[54] This change has been reflected by, among others, motivating a review process under the WTO Agreement on Trade-Related Aspects of Intellectual Property Rights ("TRIPS"), which applies to "copyright, trademarks, geographical indications, patents and undisclosed information."[55] TRIPS creates some level of harmonization between national IP regimes and

---

[50] Sara Bannerman, *The World Intellectual Property Organization and Traditional Knowledge*, in INDIGENOUS INTELLECTUAL PROPERTY: A HANDBOOK OF CONTEMPORARY RESEARCH, *supra* note 46, at 83.

[51] *Id.*

[52] *Id.* at 84; see also Stephen R. Munzer & Kal Raustiala, *The Uneasy Case for Intellectual Property Rights in Traditional Knowledge*, 27 CARDOZO ARTS & ENT. L.J. 37, 49–50 (2009) (explaining that a defensive traditional knowledge claim is one that is used to "block the enforcement of or to invalidate another variety of IP, such as a patent, owned by outsiders who used [traditional knowledge] in forging the patented invention" and that a positive protection is used if the knowledge holder wants "the economic value that would result from IP protection").

[53] *Intergovernmental Committee*, WORLD INTELL. PROP. ORG., visit http://www.wipo.int/tk/en/igc ("The WIPO Intergovernmental Committee on Intellectual Property and Genetic Resources, Traditional Knowledge and Folklore is, in accordance with its mandate, undertaking text-based negotiations with the objective of reaching agreement on a text(s) of an international legal instrument(s), which will ensure the effective protection of traditional knowledge (TK), traditional cultural expressions (TCEs) and genetic resources (GRs)").

[54] World Trade Organization *Ministerial Conference – Fourth Session – Doha, Implementation-Related Issues and Concerns* WTO Doc. WT/MIN(01)/17 (Decision of Nov. 14 2001).

[55] Agreement on Trade-Related Aspects of Intellectual Property Rights arts. 9–24, 27–34, 39, Apr. 15, 1994, Marrakesh Agreement Establishing the World Trade Organization, Annex 1C, 1869 U.N.T.S. 299, 33 I.L.M. 1197 (hereinafter TRIPS).

"minimum standards of IP" protection across its current 164 members[56] and the discussion has forced the recognition of the vulnerable position of Indigenous peoples and the possible effects of IP systems.

According to Taubman, around 2005 a "striking" evolution started also at a regional level. A significant number of bilateral and regional agreements started showing "momentum towards integration, or at least coherence, between two highly divergent areas of law and regulation," indigenous traditional knowledge and IP rights.[57] Perhaps more important – given the amount of trade and investment covered by such deals – is the inclusion in the CP-TPP, in Article 18.16, of a specific provision directing governments to cooperate in this area.[58] Jean-Frédéric Morin and Mathilde Gauquelin have surveyed "41 agreements [that] mention traditional knowledge, most often enjoining states to put into place domestic measures to ensure its protection. For instance, the agreement between Nicaragua and Taiwan calls for a protection of 'the collective intellectual property rights and the traditional knowledge of indigenous peoples and local and ethnic communities in which any of their creations ... are used commercially.'"[59]

WIPO continues to facilitate the negotiation of a series of new instruments to expand protections, including those of traditional knowledge[60] and cultural

---

[56] See Tania Voon, *The World Trade Organization, the TRIPS Agreement and Traditional Knowledge*, in Indigenous Intellectual Property: A Handbook of Contemporary Research, *supra* note 46, at 64, 67.

[57] Taubman *supra* note 49 at 377. Professor Taubman identifies thirty-three examples of such trade agreements concluded between 2003 and 2015, including agreements between EU & Colombia & Peru; Peru & Republic of Korea; Colombia & Republic of Korea; EU & CARIFORUM States; China & Costa Rica; EFTA & Colombia; EFTA & Peru; Nicaragua & Chinese Taipei; Peru & China; Guatemala & Chinese Taipei; Panama & Chinese Taipei; Switzerland & China; China & Republic of Korea; Costa Rica & Singapore; New Zealand & Malaysia; EU & Ukraine; Thailand & New Zealand; EU & Republic of Korea; Australia & China; Hong Kong China & New Zealand; Republic of Korea & New Zealand; ASEAN & Australia & New Zealand; New Zealand & Taiwan; Japan & Thailand; Canada & Panama; Canada & Peru; Economic Cooperation Organization ("ECO"); U.S. & Colombia; U.S. & Peru; Canada & Colombia; and the TransPacific Strategic Economic Partnership.

[58] CPTPP art. 18.16

[59] Jean-Frédéric Morin & Mathilde Gauquelin, "Trade Agreements as Vectors for the Nagoya Protocol's Implementation" CIGI, CIGI Papers No. 115 Nov. 2016 at 2–3, online: www .cigionline.org/sites/default/files/documents/Paper%20no.115.pdf (citing Free Trade Agreement between the Republic of China (Taiwan) and Nicaragua, June 16, 2006 (entered into force Jan. 1, 2008) art 17.17(1)).

[60] U.N. World Intellectual Property Organization, The Protection of Traditional Knowledge: Draft Articles, at 1, U.N. Doc. WIPO/GRTKF/IC/28/5 (June 2, 2014), http://www.wipo.int/ edocs/mdocs/tk/en/wipo_grtkf_ic_28/wipo_grtkf_ic_28_5.pdf.

expressions.[61] Some important indigenous scholars like James Anaya have criticized the approach. They argue that the draft documents have inherent flaws.[62] Among the most obvious are an excessive reliance on a "defensive mechanism of disclosure" (for instance, a requirement that patent applicants disclose elements of indigenous resources used in the creation of the product) and a lack of any "affirmative recognition of or specific measures of protection for Indigenous people's rights."[63] Despite these and other criticisms, WIPO has institutionalized methods to recognize the interests of Indigenous peoples, which has permeated into IP treaty-making.[64] This institutionalization – according to Taubman – "gives effect to diverse epistemologies and bodies of knowledge."[65] It also maintains the recognition of the customary law of Indigenous peoples in treaties and reinforces the legal personality of indigenous communities under international law. This in effect attempts to actualize some of the rights and aspirations of the UNDRIP, including:

> the right to maintain, control, protect and develop their cultural heritage, traditional knowledge and traditional cultural expressions, as well as the manifestations of their sciences, technologies and cultures, including human and genetic resources, seeds, medicines, knowledge of the properties of fauna and flora, oral traditions, literatures, designs, sports and traditional games and visual and performing arts [and that they] also have the right to maintain, control, protect and develop their intellectual property over such cultural heritage, traditional knowledge, and traditional cultural expressions.[66]

Overall, Taubman argues that the tensions between IP and traditional knowledge evidence the emerging use of indigenous rights first, as a point of

---

[61] U.N. World Intellectual Property Organization, The Protection of Traditional Cultural Expressions: Draft Articles, at 1, U.N. Doc WIPO/GRTKF/IC/28/6 (June 2, 2014), http://www .wipo.int/edocs/mdocs/tk/en/wipo_grtkf_ic_28/wipo_grtkf_ic_28_6.pdf.

[62] See James Anaya, U.N. World Intellectual Property Organization, Technical Review of Key Intellectual Property-Related Issues of the WIPO Draft Instruments on Genetic Resources, Traditional Knowledge and Traditional Cultural Expressions, annex at 4–6, U.N. Doc. WIPO/ GRTKF/IC/32/INF/8 (Oct. 3, 2016), http://www.wipo.int/edocs/mdocs/tk/en/wipo_grtkf_ic_32/ wipo_grtkf_ic_32_inf_8.pdf (hereinafter Technical Review). Bannerman notes that traditionally WIPO served to advance Western notions of IP. See Bannerman, *supra* note 50, at 87. Bannerman also points to at least two examples of WIPO efforts to address some of the concerns held by Indigenous peoples: the WIPO Performances and Phonogram Treaty 1996 (that protects "performances of expressions of folklore") and the Patent Cooperation Treaty 1970 (that "enhance[s] recognition of traditional knowledge as prior art"). *Id.* at 88.

[63] Technical Review, *supra Id.*, annex at 4.

[64] See Bannerman, *supra* note 50, at 104.

[65] See Taubman *supra* note 49, at 379.

[66] UN Declaration on the Rights of Indigenous Peoples, art. 31.

resistance to conventional IP norms.[67] Moreover, indigenous organizations have pressured for reform by relying on the concept of traditional knowledge. In some way, he argues, it is an embodiment of the social and economic concerns that form part of the interests that are positively asserted in trade. Notably, today at least "29 trade agreements encourage the sharing of benefits derived from the use of this knowledge."[68]

Biological and Genetic Resources: The current trend is for international economic agreements to provide more guidance regarding the circumstances and conditions of access to indigenous genetic resources – living material that includes genes of present and potential value for humans. In the view of Taubman, some of these initiatives:

> seek to rebalance the relationship between those who can provide access to traditional knowledge and genetic resources—the gatekeepers and custodians—and those who seek to benefit from access to those materials. Understanding and redefining the relationship between the providers of access, the custodians of traditional knowledge systems and genetic resources on the one hand, and the downstream users of this material on the other, is a more productive and enabling way of considering the IP issues. It offers an opportunity to move beyond the conventional structuring of IP policy, which divides the world into static binary caricatures—separating right holders and content consumers, North and South, private and public, haves and have-nots—and instead to explore a more pluralist and fluid set of rights, interests, and responsibilities in light of the intellectual and cultural riches of Indigenous peoples and traditional communities.

A notable example in that direction is the Convention on Biological Diversity ("CBD"). The CBD is designed to promote "the sustainable use and the conservation of biological diversity," and to enable "the fair and equitable sharing of benefits arising out of the utilization of genetic resources."[69] It requires state parties to adopt explicit protections for indigenous communities, including arrangements for benefit sharing.[70] While the CBD is generally

---

[67] Antony Taubman, *New Dialogues, New Pathways: Reframing the Debate on Intellectual Property and Traditional Knowledge* 58 WASHBURN L.J. (2019) 390.

[68] See Morin & Gauquelin, *supra* note 59.

[69] Convention on Biological Diversity art. 1, June 5, 1992, 1760 U.N.T.S. 79.

[70] See *id.* at preamble. The CBD recognizes "the close and traditional dependence of many indigenous and local communities embodying traditional lifestyles on biological resources, and the desirability of sharing equitably benefits arising from the use of traditional knowledge, innovations and practices relevant to the conservation of biological diversity and the sustainable use of its components." *Id.*

considered a step in the right direction,[71] some scholars argue that because the "outputs from biotechnology and industrial developments are [still] considered private property," the CBD allows for indigenous communities to be "cut off" from lucrative phases of commercialization.[72]

In order to address these and related criticisms,[73] in 2010 the governing body (representing all state parties to the treaty) adopted the Nagoya Protocol, an addition to the CBD (and other guidelines)[74] that sought to regulate the fair and equitable sharing of benefits.[75] The Nagoya Protocol expresses a commitment to "the right of indigenous and local communities to identify the rightful holders of their traditional knowledge associated with genetic resources, within their communities[.]"[76] Interestingly, the protocol requires state parties to take active measures, including domestic procedures for the identification

---

[71] See McGonigle, *supra* note 43, at 221.

[72] *Id.*

[73] See Susette Biber-Klemm & Danuta Szymura Berglas, *Problems and Goals*, in RIGHTS TO PLANT GENETIC RESOURCES AND TRADITIONAL KNOWLEDGE 3, 21 (Susette Biber-Klemm et al. eds., 2006) (criticizing the "economic orientation of the CBD").

[74] SECRETARIAT OF THE CONV. ON BIOLOGICAL DIVERSITY, NAGOYA PROTOCOL ON ACCESS TO GENETIC RESOURCES AND THE FAIR AND EQUITABLE SHARING OF BENEFITS ARISING FROM THEIR UTILIZATION TO THE CONVENTION ON BIOLOGICAL DIVERSITY (2011), https://www.cbd .int/abs/doc/protocol/nagoya-protocol-en.pdf (hereinafter NAGOYA PROTOCOL); see Convention on Biological Diversity, *supra* note 69, art. 23 (providing state parties the power to adopt protocols to the CBD). Other guidelines include the Bonn Guidelines on Access to Genetic Resources and Fair and Equitable Sharing of the Benefits Arising Out of Their Utilization. SECRETARIAT OF THE CONV. ON BIOLOGICAL DIVERSITY, BONN GUIDELINES ON ACCESS TO GENETIC RESOURCES AND FAIR AND EQUITABLE SHARING OF THE BENEFITS ARISING OUT OF THEIR UTILIZATION (2002), https://www.cbd.int/doc/publications/cbd-bonn-gdls-en.pdf. These are nonbinding provisions adopted by the COP designed to, among other things, "promote the adequate and effective transfer of appropriate technology to providing Parties, especially developing countries, in particular least developed countries and small island developing States among them, stakeholders and indigenous and local communities." *Id.* para. 11. Paul Kuruk, *Regulating Access to Traditional Knowledge and Genetic Resources: The Disclosure Requirement as a Strategy to Combat Biopiracy*, 17 SAN DIEGO INT'L L.J. 1, 21–2 (2015). At the WIPO, some actions are also addressing similar concerns. See U.N. World Intellectual Property Organization, Consolidated Document Relating to Intellectual Property and Genetic Resources, at 6, U.N. Doc. WIPO/GRTKF/IC/34/4 (Mar. 15, 2017), http://www.wipo.int/ meetings/en/doc_details.jsp?doc_id=368344 (stated goal: to prevent the misappropriation or patenting of resources). For discussion, see Achmad Gusman Siswandi, *The Nagoya Protocol: Unfinished Business Remains Unfinished*, in INDIGENOUS INTELLECTUAL PROPERTY: A HANDBOOK OF CONTEMPORARY RESEARCH, *supra* note 46, at 334, 337 (arguing that the Nagoya Protocol "marks a new chapter" regarding access and benefit sharing).

[75] Convention on Biological Diversity, *Decision Adopted by the Conference of the Parties to the Convention on Biological Diversity at Its Tenth Meeting*, U.N. Doc. UNEP/CBD/DEC/X/1, annex I (Oct. 29, 2010).

[76] NAGOYA PROTOCOL, *supra* note 74, at preamble.

of holders of rights associated with genetic resources.[77] Overall, the main concern with the Nagoya Protocol seems to be its reach: it is solely aimed at deterrence as there is limited enforcement available for its provisions.[78]

Related to the CBD, the 2001 International Treaty on Plant Genetic Resources for Food and Agriculture provides similar protections for indigenous communities.[79] This framework is concerned with "farmers' rights," but applies indirectly to indigenous communities that rely on subsistence agriculture. Designed to provide for the "conservation and sustainable use of plant genetic resources for food and agriculture," this treaty is meant to operate in harmony with the CBD.[80] It places obligations on states to adopt legislation, rather than creating self-executing obligations.[81] Ultimately, the genetic resources treaty is similar to the CBD in that it mandates the fair and equitable sharing of benefits[82] and is designed to incorporate many of the CBD's provisions into the agricultural sector.[83] The European Union, Colombia and Peru have also entered in a trade agreement that devotes a

---

[77] See *id.* art. 21.

[78] See *id.* art. 30. Kuruk instead proposes a disclosure requirement that would force those applying for patents to indicate whether "a claimed invention was based on or derived from traditional knowledge or genetic resources." Kuruk, *supra* note 74, at 36. See also KEITH AOKI, SEED WARS 86 n.113 (2008) (noting that previous international regimes, such as the International Treaty on Plant Genetic Resources (ITPGR), also left implementation of the treaties to national governments). While the Nagoya Protocol is, on the whole, a step in the right direction, many shortcomings have been noted by indigenous rights experts. See generally World Intellectual Property Organization, Nagoya Protocol on Access and Benefit Sharing: Substantive and Procedural Injustices Relating to Indigenous Peoples' Human Rights 4, (July 11–15, 2011), https://www.wipo.int/export/sites/www/tk/en/documents/pdf/grand_council_of_the_crees_annex_comments_on_observer_participation.pdf.

[79] See Peter-Tobias Stoll & Anja von Hahn, *Indigenous Peoples, Indigenous Knowledge and Indigenous Resources in International Law*, in INDIGENOUS HERITAGE AND INTELLECTUAL PROPERTY: GENETIC RESOURCES, TRADITIONAL KNOWLEDGE AND FOLKLORE 7, 42 (Silke von Lewinski ed., 2nd ed. 2008).

[80] Plant Genetic Resources for Food and Agriculture art. 1, Nov. 3, 2001, T.I.A.S. No. 17–313; see also *id.* art. 9.3 ("Nothing in this Article shall be interpreted to limit any rights that farmers have to save, use, exchange and sell farm-saved seed/propagating material, subject to national law and as appropriate"). The term "farmer" may include many indigenous communities primarily involved in this activity. *Id.* art 9.1.

[81] See *id.* art. 4.

[82] See Colombia-US, *Exchange of Letter and China-Costa Rica Free Trade Agreement of 2010*, art. 111 in Jean-Frédéric Morin, *Trade and Environment Database (TREND)* at 50. Visit https://www.chaire-epi.ulaval.ca/sites/chaire-epi.ulaval.ca/files/codebook.pdf OR for the China-Costa Rica Agreement visit https://investmentpolicy.unctad.org/international-investment-agreements/treaty-files/2608/download.

[83] See H. David Cooper, *The International Treaty on Plant Genetic Resources for Food and Agriculture*, 11 RECIEL 1, 15 (2002); Stoll & Hahn, *supra* note 79, at 41–4.

full chapter to the protection of biodiversity and traditional knowledge.[84] In addition, the agreement on the environment entered between Canada and Colombia has also addressed Indigenous peoples' issues – signatory parties have reiterated their commitment as established by the CBD. Hence, it is fair to adduce that these positive trends add to the reinforcement of the obligations under the CBD.[85]

So far, all these efforts have advanced a movement for the recalibration of economic interests of Indigenous peoples that has permeated the work of the WTO. For instance, during the last decade and under the aegis of the concerns of sustainable development raised by the Doha Declaration, the WTO deliberates how "the patent system should take account of, or otherwise link to, the obligations that a user of traditional knowledge and genetic resources assumes when accessing and exploiting these materials."[86] Again at the regional level, many examples of this impact include the 2011 Trade Agreement between the EU, Colombia and Peru (to which Ecuador subsequently acceded) provided:

(1) The Parties recognise the importance and value of biological diversity and its components and of the associated traditional knowledge, innovations and practices of indigenous and local communities. The Parties furthermore reaffirm their sovereign rights over their natural resources and recognise their rights and obligations as established by the CBD with respect to access to genetic resources, and to the fair and equitable sharing of benefits arising out of the utilization of these genetic resources.

---

[84] See Trade Agreement between the European Union and Its Member States, of the One Part, and Colombia and Peru, of the Other Part, chapter 2, https://trade.ec.europa.eu/doclib/docs/2011/march/tradoc_147704.pdf.

[85] See Agreement on the Environment between Canada and the Republic of Colombia, art. 5 https://www.canada.ca/content/dam/eccc/migration/main/caraib-carib/ffef249c-faae-450d-80ce-dd48f8d48cad/colombia_agreement_e.pdf OR see Jean-Frédéric Morin *Trade and Environment Database (TREND)* at 50, https://www.chaire-epi.ulaval.ca/sites/chaire-epi.ulaval.ca/files/codebook.pdf.

[86] See, e.g., Trade Negots. Committee, Rep. by the Director-General: Issues Related to the Extension of the Protection of Geographical Indications Provided for in Article 23 of the TRIPS Agreement to Products Other Than Wines and Spirits and Those Related to the Relationship between the TRIPS Agreement and the Convention on Biological Diversity, WTO Doc. TN/C/W/61 (Apr. 21, 2011); Trade Negots. Committee, Draft Decision to Enhance Mutual Supportiveness between the TRIPS Agreement and the Convention on Biological Diversity, WTO Doc. TN/C/W/59 (Apr. 19, 2011), (https://perma.cc/DL97-YPS3) (proposal by Brazil, China, Colombia, Ecuador, India, Indonesia, Peru, Thailand, the ACP Group and the African Group).

Like the traditional knowledge debate, the IP-CBD debate pivots on the question of what recognition, if any, intellectual property law systems might be required to give to the circumstances of access to, and use of, genetic resources of Indigenous peoples. This results in key questions for indigenous rights advocates that also affect other forms of IP protections. In any event, it seems clear that such access to genetic resources should be subject to prior informed consent.[87]

Trademarks, Patents and Geographical Indications: Indigenous peoples can also rely on national IP regimes to guard their creations, but these regimes seldom offer Indigenous peoples tailored protection. Recently, a commentator has explained that "the requirements and limitations built into trademark law make it particularly difficult . . . to protect [indigenous] cultural products, [and that] trademark law is largely ineffective for, or even counterproductive to, the deterrence of cultural appropriation."[88] Even so, to the extent that national IP regimes *can* protect cultural resources, the TRIPS Agreement has some indirect application.[89]

The TRIPS Agreement includes no special protections for Indigenous peoples.[90] However, the provisions can be used for recognizing Indigenous peoples rights, including collective marks (with potential extension to protect collective personality), traditional processes and suppression of unfair competition such as false claims of indigenous authenticity. One key aspect of this usage, as Taubman explains, is that indigenous protections seek "ways of ensuring an equitable and fair form of IP that does evolve with time and does take account of intergenerational factors."[91] However, IP rights tend to be consciously or deliberately time-bound, hence protecting only one generation

---

[87] See Free Trade Agreement between the Republic of Colombia and the EFTA States, art. 6.5.7, https://www.efta.int/media/documents/legal-texts/free-trade-relations/colombia/EFTA-Colombia%20Free%20Trade%20Agreement%20EN.pdf.

[88] Sari Sharoni, *The Mark of a Culture: The Efficacy and Propriety of Using Trademark Law to Deter Cultural Appropriation*, Stan. L. Sch. 35 (Sept. 6, 2016), https://law.stanford.edu/publications/the-mark-of-a-culture-the-efficiency-and-propriety-of-using-trademark-law-to-deter-cultural-appropriatio.

[89] TRIPS *supra* note 55.

[90] Stoll & Hahn, *supra* note 79, at 37. Among international trade law specialists, there is debate regarding the extent of application of GATT Article XX exceptions to TRIPS. These exceptions could be used to excuse violations of the encompassed legal agreements when protecting other values, including the interest of indigenous peoples. See Chang-fa Lo, *Potential Conflict between TRIPS and GATT concerning Parallel Importation of Drugs and Possible Solution to Prevent Undesirable Market Segmentation*, 66 Food & Drug L.J. 73, 80 (2011); Yenkong Ngangjoh-Hodu, *Relationship of Gatt Article XX Exceptions to Other WTO Agreements*, 80 Nordic J. Int'l L. 219, 230–34 (2011).

[91] Taubman *supra* note 67, at 386

or product cycle. This forces Indigenous peoples to be creative to find protections within the traditional IP system.

Of particular utility is one of the protective tools explicitly outlined under the TRIPS: geographical indications. This form of protection can be employed to protect tribal resources in different ways. Geographical indications protect the names, "which identify a good as originating in the territory of a Member, or a region or locality in that territory."[92] Hence, if officially recognized, geographical indications can prevent outside exploitation, generic imitations and unfair appropriation of indigenous resources. The problem is that the decision involving what products to protect under geographical indication is often not free of political considerations.

Moreover, TRIPS Article 27 allows for member states to exclude "plants and animals other than micro-organisms, and essentially biological processes" from patentability.[93] Based on this provision, domestic legislations can exclude from patentability certain forms of knowledge and processes. While some aspects of this Article are unclear, at minimum, it can be employed to protect against illegitimate appropriation of biological and genetic resources and traditional knowledge if read in a consistent manner with the WIPO and the CBD agreements.[94] Some argue that this overlap leaves ambiguity regarding the extent of the legal obligations and "allow[s] different states to take different views on the matter."[95]

The discussions within the WTO about patentability and indigenous resources have had practical effects, even if they are not reflected in the legal text of the TRIPS Agreement. In essence, they have led to "a broader, and culturally and epistemologically more diverse, base of prior art that is routinely consulted in patent examination procedures." Reflecting this, the CP-TPP

---

[92] TRIPS, *supra* note 55, art. 22.

[93] *Id.* art. 27(3)(b).

[94] Part of the problem is that Article 27 states that members "shall provide for the protection of plant varieties either by patents or by an effective *sui generis* system or by any combination thereof." *Id.* See generally GEOGRAPHICAL INDICATIONS AT THE CROSSROADS OF TRADE, DEVELOPMENT, AND CULTURE: FOCUS ON ASIA-PACIFIC (Irene Calboli & Ng-Loy Wee Loon eds., 2017).

[95] Susette Biber-Klemm et al., *The Current Law of Plant Genetic Resources and Traditional Knowledge*, in RIGHTS TO PLANT GENETIC RESOURCES AND TRADITIONAL KNOWLEDGE, *supra* note 73, at 56, 62; see AOKI, *supra* note 75, at 83. In addition to TRIPS, many other bilateral and multilateral investment and trade agreements contain IP provisions or protect IP protections from unreasonable regulation. These provisions, known as TRIPS-Plus, often require states to put protections in place that are even greater than those found in TRIPS. Like TRIPS, TRIPS-Plus provisions tend to ignore any type of collective rights. See generally Susan K. Sell, *TRIPS Was Never Enough: Vertical Forum Shifting, FTAS, ACTA, and TPP*, 18 J. INTELL. PROP. L. 447 (2011).

explicitly mandates that in the examination of patent applications the authorities should implement culturally appropriate quality patent examination. To achieve that, the process may include:

(a) that in determining prior art, relevant publicly available documented information related to traditional knowledge associated with genetic resources may be taken into account;

(b) an opportunity for third parties to cite, in writing, to the competent examining authority prior art disclosures that may have a bearing on patentability, including prior art disclosures related to traditional knowledge associated with genetic resources;

(c) if applicable and appropriate, the use of databases or digital libraries containing traditional knowledge associated with genetic resources; and

(d) cooperation in the training of patent examiners in the examination of patent applications related to traditional knowledge associated with genetic resources.[96]

Intangible Cultural Heritage & Folklore: Finally, protections for indigenous property, including intangible property, have been established in international treaties dealing with cultural heritage.[97] While other economic treaties recognize ownership over indigenous intangible heritage and expressions to varying degrees,[98] the Convention on the Protection and Promotion of the Diversity of Cultural Expressions is the most explicit and comprehensive.[99] This 2005 UNESCO treaty mandates its state parties to enact a broad range of measures to protect indigenous cultural heritage, including licensing restrictions, quotas

---

[96] CP-TPP 18.6.

[97] See Convention Respecting the Laws and Customs of War on Land arts. 23, 28, 46–7, 56, Oct. 18, 1907, 36 Stat. 2277, 1 Bevans 631; Convention for the Protection of Cultural Property in the Event of Armed Conflict arts. 1–4, May 14, 1954, 249 U.N.T.S. 240; Convention on the Means of Prohibiting and Preventing the Illicit Import, Export and Transfer of Ownership of Cultural Property arts.1–2, Nov. 14, 1970, 823 U.N.T.S. 231.

[98] See for instance, New Zealand – Hong Kong, China Closer Economic Partnership Agreement of 2010, Chapter 11, Art. 8, ("Subject to the international obligations that are applicable to each Party, each Party may establish appropriate measures to protect genetic resources, traditional knowledge and traditional cultural expressions or folklore"), https://investmentpolicy.unctad.org/international-investment-agreements/treaty-files/2600/download.

[99] See generally UNESCO General Conference, Convention on the Protection and Promotion of the Diversity of Cultural Expressions, U.N. Doc. CLT-2005/Convention Diversite-Cult Rev.2 (Oct. 20, 2005) (hereinafter 2005 Convention). For a more detailed discussion on trade and cultural heritage, see generally Tania Voon, *Substantive WTO Law and the Convention on the Diversity of Cultural Expression*, in THE UNESCO CONVENTION ON THE DIVERSITY OF CULTURAL EXPRESSIONS: A TALE OF FRAGMENTATION IN INTERNATIONAL LAW 273 (Toshiyuki Kono & Steven Van Uytsel eds., 2012).

and preferential treatment. It also creates the International Fund for Cultural Diversity to promote sustainable development and poverty alleviation for vulnerable groups – regrettably without a funding mandate.[100] Notably, the Convention states that nothing under its terms shall be interpreted as "modifying rights and obligations of the Parties under any other treaties to which they are parties." This text was included, in part, anticipating possible tensions with trade obligations under the WTO Agreements.[101]

At the regional level, some language to protect folklore and cultural heritage has been included. Notably, the 2004 FTA between Taiwan and Panama contained specific obligations. These provisions not only explicitly articulate a norm against misappropriation through the IP system, but also emphasize the indigenous sociological and cultural values and the need to create avenues for justice for indigenous groups. In the relevant part, the treaty states:

(2) Each Party shall recognize that the customs, traditions, beliefs, spirituality, religiosity, cosmos vision, folklore expressions, artistic manifestations, traditional skills and any other form of traditional expression of the Indigenous people and local communities are a part of their cultural heritage.

(3) The cultural heritage shall not be subject to any form of exclusivity by unauthorized third parties applying the intellectual property system, unless the request is done by the Indigenous people and local communities or by third parties with their authorization.[102]

* * *

---

[100] Michael Hahn, *A Clash of Cultures? The UNESCO Diversity Convention and International Trade Law*, 9 J. Int'l Econ. L. 515, 537 (2006).

[101] *Id.* at 543; see also Mary E. Footer & Christopher Beat Graber, *Trade Liberalization and Cultural Policy*, 3 J. Int'l Econ. L. 115, 122–26 (2000).

[102] Free Trade Agreement between the Republic of China and the Republic of Panama, Pan.-Taiwan, art. 16.05, Jan. 1, 2004, https://wits.worldbank.org/GPTAD/PDF/archive/Panama-Taiwan.pdf (https://perma.cc/PH68-UQX9). See also Trade Agreement between the European Union and its Member States, of the One Part, and Colombia and Peru, of the Other Part, art. 201, (section 3 of such article reads: "Subject to their domestic legislation, the Parties shall, in accordance with Article 8(j) of the CBD respect, preserve and maintain knowledge, innovations and practices of indigenous and local communities embodying traditional lifestyles relevant for the conservation and sustainable use of biological diversity, and promote their wider application conditioned to the prior informed consent of the holders of such knowledge, innovations and practices, and encourage the equitable sharing of the benefits arising from the utilization of such knowledge, innovations and practices"), https://trade.ec.europa.eu/doclib/docs/2011/march/tradoc_147704.pdf

In short, multiple difficulties are associated with incorporating indigenous protections into international IP regimes. These include the use of the public domain; the incorporation of collective ownership; the consideration of inter-generational factors; the separation of commercial values from cultural values; and the differing concepts of property and value in general. These difficulties have yet to be adequately considered in the agreements, some of which provide limited *sui generis* protections for Indigenous peoples. Nevertheless, perhaps in no other area of international economic law has the debate over how best to accommodate the rights and interests of Indigenous peoples been more vibrant – especially around the IP concept of traditional knowledge. This has led to the adoption of exceptions to general rules that prevent the misuse of the IP of Indigenous peoples and, in more limited cases, positive protections granted through rules to enforce domestically such rights that focus primarily on consent and economic benefits. As one of the leading voices in the interconnection of IP and indigenous rights declared, the debates brought to the international economic system:

> wider issues of governance, equity, and legitimacy in recognizing the role and status of Indigenous and local communities more generally;

> the cultural and axiological settings that underpin and shape international and multilateral governance systems; and

> the interests and values that these systems recognize and potentially privilege.[103]

3.2.2 *Finance*

Multilateral and regional development banks such as the WBG, the Asian Development Bank ("ADB") and the Inter-American Development Bank ("IDB") provide capital for development projects – such as resource extraction or large infrastructure projects – that ultimately impact Indigenous peoples.[104] Over time, procedures designed to ensure compliance with indigenous rights and to hear the concerns of Indigenous peoples have been adopted. These rights are incorporated as "safeguards" via lending agreements signed between institutions and states, subnational entities or even private MNCs (through

---

[103] *Taubman supra* note 67.
[104] Andrew Gray, *Development Policy – Development Protest: The World Bank, Indigenous Peoples, and NGOs*, in THE STRUGGLE FOR ACCOUNTABILITY: THE WORLD BANK, NGOs, AND GRASSROOTS MOVEMENTS 267, 268 (Jonathan A. Fox & L. David Brown eds., 1998).

entities like IFC) which are recipients of the financing.[105] The main goal of these standards is to "Ensure that there is no prejudice or discrimination toward project-affected individuals or communities and to give particular consideration to Indigenous peoples, minority groups, and those disadvantaged or vulnerable, especially where adverse impacts may arise or development benefits are to be shared."[106]

The path to include safeguards in lending agreements has not been straightforward. After a series of pitfalls and controversies, the WBG has been a leader in this field. Among other examples of impacts, the WBG funded the Chixoy dam in Guatemala. Despite flooding the territory of nearby Mayan communities, the dam was constructed without any finalized plans on resettlement and compensation to the indigenous population. When residents began to protest, the Guatemalan government used force, allegedly killing several members of the community. Also relevant is a conflict that resulted from the Pangue project that catalyzed the strengthening of the WBG's institutional capacity to address issues of this nature. The conflict also resulted from the flooding of the land of Indigenous Pehuenche communities.[107]

The evolution of the safeguards at the WBG can be summarized as follows: In the eighties, it issued the first policy specifically dedicated to Indigenous peoples.[108] In the nineties, the WBG adopted a directive that sought to "ensure that the development process fosters full respect" for indigenous rights

---

[105] See, e.g., INTER-AM. DEV. BANK, OPERATIONAL POLICY ON INDIGENOUS PEOPLES AND STRATEGY FOR INDIGENOUS DEVELOPMENT 6 (2006), http://idbdocs.iadb.org/wsdocs/getdocument.aspx?docnum=2032081; INT'L FIN. CORP., OVERVIEW OF PERFORMANCE STANDARDS ON ENVIRONMENTAL AND SOCIAL SUSTAINABILITY 1 (2012), https://www.ifc.org/wps/wcm/connect/1ee7038049a79139b845faa8c6a8312a/PS7_English_2012.pdf?MOD=AJPERES.

[106] WORLD BANK GROUP, WORLD BANK ENVIRONMENTAL AND SOCIAL FRAMEWORK: SETTING ENVIRONMENTAL AND SOCIAL STANDARDS FOR INVESTMENT PROJECT FINANCING (2016), p. 2 http://documents.worldbank.org/curated/en/383011492423734099/pdf/114278-WP-REVISED-PUBLIC-Environmental-and-Social-Framework.pdf. This Policy replaces among other Operational Policies ("OP") and Bank Procedures ("BP"): OP/BP4.10, Indigenous Peoples, OP/BP4.11, Physical Cultural Resources, OP/BP4.12, Involuntary Resettlement, OP/BP4.36, Forests and OP/BP4.37, Safety of Dams.

[107] Barbara Rose Johnston, *Chixoy Dam Legacies: The Struggle to Secure Reparation and the Right to Remedy in Guatemala*, 3 WATER ALTERNATIVES 341, 342–43 (2010). See International Finance Corporation, *Lessons Learned: Pangue Hydroelectric* (Sept. 2008), https://www.ifc.org/wps/wcm/connect/topics_ext_content/ifc_external_corporate_site/sustainability-at-ifc/publications/publications_loe_pangue__wci__1319578750067.

[108] Navin Rai, Implementation of the World Bank's Indigenous Peoples Policy: A Learning Review (FY 2006–2008) 1 (2011), http://documents.worldbank.org/curated/en/427941468163488772/pdf/647570WP0Box360s0review0august02011.pdf.

and culture.[109] The directive required borrowers for investment projects affecting Indigenous peoples to "prepare an Indigenous peoples' development plan;"[110] work to recognize "the customary or traditional land tenure systems;"[111] and incorporate indigenous communities in the decision-making process.[112] In 2005, the directive was revised and an *Operational Policy on Indigenous Peoples* (or "OP/BP 4.10") was replaced in 2016 by the WBG's *Environmental and Social Framework or 2016 ESF* – these two frameworks incorporated vast protections for Indigenous peoples.[113]

The current framework links different topics relevant for indigenous communities *transversally*, but it is the Standard 7 that is directly applicable to indigenous peoples/Sub-Saharan African Historically Underserved Traditional Local Communities. The framework applies whenever Indigenous peoples (as they may be referred to in the national context) are present in, or have collective attachment to a proposed project area, as determined during the environmental and social assessment. It applies regardless of whether the indigenous communities are affected positively or negatively, and regardless of the significance of any such impacts. It also applies irrespective of the presence or absence of *discernible* economic, political or social vulnerabilities. Two particularly relevant objectives of Standard 7 include:

- To improve project design and promote local support by establishing and maintaining an ongoing relationship based on meaningful consultation with the Indigenous peoples/Sub-Saharan African Historically Underserved Traditional Local Communities affected by a project throughout the project's life cycle.

    . . .

---

[109] THE WORLD BANK, THE WORLD BANK OPERATIONAL MANUAL, OPERATIONAL DIRECTIVE 4.20: INDIGENOUS PEOPLES para. 6 (Sept. 1991), https://www.ifc.org/wps/wcm/connect/ 835cc5004885527oab94fb6a6515bb18/OD420_IndigenousPeoples.pdf?MOD=AJPERES.

[110] *Id.* para. 13.

[111] *Id.* para. 15(c).

[112] *Id.* para. 15(d).

[113] WORLD BANK GROUP, WORLD BANK ENVIRONMENTAL AND SOCIAL FRAMEWORK: SETTING ENVIRONMENTAL AND SOCIAL STANDARDS FOR INVESTMENT PROJECT FINANCING (2016), http:// documents.worldbank.org/curated/en/383011492423734099/pdf/114278-WP-REVISED-PUBLIC-Environmental-and-Social-Framework.pdf disclosure_post_board_august_4.pdf. This Policy replaces among other Operational Policies ("OP") and Bank Procedures ("BP"): OP/ BP4.10, Indigenous Peoples, OP/BP4.11, Physical Cultural Resources, OP/BP4.12, Involuntary Resettlement, OP/BP4.36, Forests and OP/BP4.37, Safety of Dams. The ESF become effective in Oct. 2018.

- To obtain the Free, Prior and Informed Consent (FPIC) of affected Indigenous peoples/Sub-Saharan African Historically Underserved Traditional Local Communities in the three circumstances described in this ESS.

Notably, under the current policy, borrowers have the duty to engage in "free, prior and informed" consultation,[114] as well as to avoid "adverse impacts" on indigenous communities or FPIC.[115] This duty to consult can be seen as being instrumental to "mitigate the adverse effects of the structure and operation of the international legal order" – a legal order that generally upholds the decision-making power of states within their respective ambits of recognized sovereignty and not Indigenous peoples. There are other sources that bound states to implement FPIC, including the International Labour Organization's Convention no. 169 Concerning Indigenous and Tribal Peoples in Independent Countries (Convention no. 169). This treaty is widely ratified in Latin America and embodies the international legal duty to carry out consultations "whenever consideration is being given to legislative or administrative measures which may affect [Indigenous peoples] directly." Similarly, the United Nations (UN) Declaration on the Rights of Indigenous peoples requires that "states consult in good faith with the Indigenous peoples concerned in order to obtain their free, prior and informed consent, before adopting and implementing legislative or administrative measures that may affect them."[116] As I have explained with Anaya elsewhere: Consultations,

> must be implemented with due consideration to Indigenous peoples' historical struggles and seek at all times to avoid additional aggravations. This requires specific interpretative choices, which are mainly to construct legal norms in a manner that is most advantageous to the enjoyment of human rights (a *pro homine* principle) when conflicting interests are at issue. In practical terms, this also means that the maximum enjoyment of human rights is typically achieved if the process focuses on reaching agreement on terms that are fair and just from a human rights perspective and not merely on obtaining consent (on whatever terms).[117]

---

[114] *Id.* at 21.
[115] *Id.* at 32–3.
[116] UN Declaration on the Rights of Indigenous Peoples, art. 19.
[117] S. James Anaya & Sergio Puig, *Mitigating State Sovereignty: The Duty to Consult with Indigenous Peoples*, 67 U. Toronto L.J. 435, 439–46 (2017) (hereinafter Mitigating State Sovereignty).

In addition to standards applied to "[p]rojects designed solely to benefit Indigenous peoples," the framework set standards when Indigenous peoples "are not the sole beneficiaries." The first type is (when sole beneficiaries) require, among other things, that the bank ensures the "ownership and participation in project design, implementation, monitoring and evaluation" of the indigenous community. The second type includes "avoidance of adverse impacts," risk mitigation, the development of community benefits and meaningful consultation as well as culturally appropriate and accessible grievance mechanisms. A breach of these standards, including the failure to consult, can result in accountability proceedings, remedial plans of different sorts and canceling loan disbursements and sanctions (as a last resort) through the inspection panel of the WBG – a mechanism for grievance redress and accountability that has analogous compliance systems under other development financial institutions.[118]

Efforts to establish safeguards in financing (and similar) agreements have been mirrored or expanded upon in other institutions. For instance, the ADB's *Safeguard Policy Statement* requires the bank to "implement projects in a way that fosters full respect for Indigenous peoples' identity, dignity, human rights, livelihood systems, and cultural uniqueness."[119] The IDB's *Operational Policy on Indigenous Peoples and Strategy for Indigenous Development* is designed "to prevent or minimize exclusion and adverse impacts . . . [on] Indigenous peoples and their rights."[120] Other similar bodies in the business of international development finance, like the US Agency for

---

[118] *Id.* at 22; According to the framework, "[p]roject-affected parties may submit complaints regarding a Bank-financed project to the project grievance mechanism, appropriate local grievance mechanism, or the World Bank's corporate Grievance Redress Service (GRS). The GRS ensures that complaints received are promptly reviewed in order to address project-related concerns. After bringing their concerns directly to the World Bank's attention and giving Bank Management a reasonable opportunity to respond, project-affected parties may submit their complaint to the World Bank's independent Inspection Panel to request an inspection to determine whether harm has occurred as a direct result of World Bank noncompliance with its policies and procedures." *Id.* p. 11 see *Panama Land Administration Project: World Bank Approves Action Plan after Reviewing Inspection Panel Findings*, WORLD BANK (Feb. 4, 2011), http://www.worldbank.org/en/news/press-release/2011/02/04/panama-land-administration-project-world-bank-approves-action-plan-after-reviewing-inspection-panel-findings. One recent example of a compliance action involved the Naso and Ngäbe peoples of Panama. There, the WBG's Inspection Panel investigated a project designed to simplify and modernize Panama's land registration system. After finding that the project managers had failed to prepare an Indigenous Peoples Development Plan, they were required to create a compliance plan, which was later adopted by the WBG. *Id.*

[119] ASIAN DEV. BANK, SAFEGUARD POLICY STATEMENT 55 (2009), https://www.adb.org/sites/default/files/institutional-document/32056/safeguard-policy-statement-june2009.pdf.

[120] INTER-AM. DEV. BANK, *supra* note 105, art. 4.

International Development or Japan's International Cooperation Agency, have similar protections and enforcement processes.[121] According to some, however, the recent emergence of new financial institutions – namely the Asian Infrastructure Investment Bank or AIIB – threatens to erode the near universality of these protections.[122]

Despite this concern, the AIIB has adopted standards similar to other IFIs – for now.[123] In particular the Environmental and Social Standard 3, includes similar provisions to Standard 7 of ESF. Among them, the AIIB must ensure "To design and implement Projects in a way that fosters full respect for Indigenous peoples' identity, dignity, human rights, economies and cultures, as defined by the Indigenous peoples themselves, so that they: (a) receive culturally appropriate social and economic benefits; (b) do not suffer adverse impacts as a result of Projects; and (c) can participate actively in Projects that affect them." The problem remains in the accountability process to ensure the correct application of the framework. Currently, it happens via an "oversight mechanism" of recent creation and without a track record.

Though safeguards are generally incorporated in lending (think of IFC or AIIB), guarantees (think of The Multilateral Investment Guarantee Agency (**MIGA**)) and other financial instruments like export promotion (think of **Export–Import Bank** of the United States or EXIM Bank) agreements, their efficacy has been questioned, especially in light of the often broad scope of exceptions to the adopted standards. Even at the WBG, these safeguards may "on an exceptional basis, with prior agreement of the Bank, and where the Borrower demonstrates that all reasonable efforts to resolve such matters have been taken," be bypassed. Moreover, several cases have been brought to the compliance bodies of these institutions to investigate failures to comply correctly with safeguards.[124] Another core weakness is that if a violation is found, it triggers an investigation that can lead to remedial actions, including

---

[121] See Caribbean Dev. Bank, Guidelines for the Social Analysis of Development Projects ¶ 3.08 (2004), http://www.caribank.org/uploads/2013/11/C4.2-SIA_Guidelines_2004.pdf; African Dev. Bank, Development and Indigenous Peoples in Africa 3 (2016), https://www.afdb.org/fileadmin/uploads/afdb/Documents/Publications/Development_and_Indigenous_Peoples_in_Africa__En__-__v3_.pdf.

[122] See ALEX MOURANT ET AL., ENSURING SUSTAINABILITY IN THE ASIAN INFRASTRUCTURE INVESTMENT BANK AND THE NEW DEVELOPMENT BANK 21–2 (2015).

[123] See Asian Infrastructure Inv. Bank, Environmental and Social Framework 42–5 (2016), https://www.aiib.org/en/policies-strategies/_download/environment-framework/20160226043633542.pdf.

[124] E.g., Inter-Am. Dev. Bank, Mexico-Mareña Renovables Wind Project, ME-MICI002–2012 (Dec. 26, 2012), https://www.iadb.org/en/mici/complaint-detail-2014,1804.html?id=ME-MICI002-2012 ("The Requesters also alleged that the harm was caused in part by the Bank's failure to request an evaluation of the adverse effects on the indigenous communities and its

the cancellation of disbursements and possibly, the temporary or permanent suspension of eligibility to participate in future projects – not necessary compliance with obligations toward Indigenous peoples. Additionally, some hold that institutions have either failed or refused to "discipline either governments or [MNCs] for violating the [safeguards]."[125] Finally, important criticisms include the failure of the safeguards to link explicitly the substantive and procedural requirements to other, more robust sources of international legal authority.[126] These links could strengthen protections and ultimately incorporate human rights obligations derived from customary international law in an expansive way.

In a comprehensive study conducted by the Inspection Panel of the WBG, the international body assessed some of these criticisms. Relying on a case study methodology the report's main conclusions included that:[127]

- Greater expertise needs to be deployed to capture the specificities of Indigenous peoples, their livelihoods, and cultural attachment to lands

---

failure to consider the same communities as potential beneficiaries of the Project to be developed on their lands"); Inter-Am. Dev. Bank, Rural Land Titling & Registration Project in Peru: Third Phase (PTRT-3), MICI-PE-2015-0094 (Aug. 27, 2015), https://idblegacy.iadb.org/en/mici/mici-word,20069. html?ID=MICI-PE-2015-0094&isAjaxRequest ("Specifically, the Requesters believed that project will violate their property owner's rights and the use of the indigenous territories, by allocating the titles in the first instance to colonists").

[125] Edmund Terence Gomez & Suzana Sawyer, *State, Capital, Multinational Institutions, and Indigenous Peoples*, in THE POLITICS OF RESOURCE EXTRACTION: INDIGENOUS PEOPLES, MULTINATIONAL CORPORATIONS, AND THE STATE 33, 35 (Edmund Terence Gomez & Suzana Sawyer eds., 2012). According to other authors, IFIs still limit their "involvement in future projects in the country from fear of further noncompliance" and staff of the organizations "who fail to enforce the standards are subject to investigation by [the internal accountability mechanisms]." Galit A. Sarfaty, *The World Bank and the Internalization of Indigenous Rights Norms*, 114 YALE L.J. 1791, 1799 (2005) (citing Benedict Kingsbury, *Operational Policies of International Institutions as Part of the Law-Making Process: The World Bank and Indigenous Peoples*, in THE REALITY OF INTERNATIONAL LAW: ESSAYS IN HONOUR OF IAN BROWNLIE 323, 330–32, 338–39 (Guy S. Goodwin-Gill & Stefan Talmon eds., 1999)).

[126] Daniel D. Bradlow, *The Reform of the Governance of the IFIs: A Critical Assessment*, in THE WORLD BANK LEGAL REVIEW: INTERNATIONAL FINANCIAL INSTITUTIONS AND GLOBAL LEGAL GOVERNANCE 37, 52 (Hassane Cissé et al. eds., 2012) (stating "it is striking that the MDBs' policies do not explicitly reference either the applicable international legal standards or the applicable decisions, declaration, or other legal instruments of those institutions and bodies").

[127] Emerging lessons series, http://documents.worldbank.org/curated/en/447361478156710826/pdf/109710-REVISED-PUBLIC-IP-lessons-text-10-31-16web-links.pdf (according to the report the method included: "A complete review of the Panel's database led to the initial identification of the main issues arising in projects involving Indigenous Peoples. Of the Panel's 34 investigated cases, 18 have involved Indigenous Peoples (see Appendix B). While all of these cases were studied for the purposes of this report, emphasis was placed on the lessons from cases within the past 10 years").

and resources. This points to the need for strengthened technical capacity and continued capacity development for relevant Bank staff.

- The World Bank has responded positively to many of the Panel investigations by adjusting its practices and increasing attention to indigenous issues on the part of borrowers. For example, in the Democratic Republic of Congo (DRC), the Panel case led to the recognition of Pygmies as Indigenous peoples by both the government and the World Bank, resulting in new commitments to mainstreaming Indigenous peoples as a crosscutting theme across activities in the country, as well as community-managed forest concessions granted to [Indigenous peoples]. In the Kenya Natural Resource Management Project (NRMP) and as a result of the Panel's investigation, the Bank hosted a dialogue with the government and affected [Indigenous peoples] on customary land and resource rights with the aim of addressing legacy issues related to land rights and ownership.

Despite the opposite sentiment of some human rights scholars as to the effect on development projects,[128] there is wide agreement that safeguards have played a major role in the development of indigenous protections worldwide.[129] Two effects are often considered. First, as international organizations "influence their member states" they can pressure governments to deal more effectively with indigenous rights as well as to include Indigenous peoples in the development priorities.[130] Second, the efforts to implement social safeguards have led to the adoption of similar efforts by private lenders and to raise awareness of the importance of IFIs in the materialization of human rights. One examples of private efforts in this area is the Equator Principles, a set of guidelines based on the WBG policies that seek to increase public accountability of private lenders.[131]

---

[128] Some have noted the failure of the World Bank to put requirements for "free, prior, and informed consent" into its operational policies and its use of the term "consultation" instead. S. J. ROMBOUTS, HAVING A SAY: INDIGENOUS PEOPLES, INTERNATIONAL LAW AND FREE, PRIOR AND INFORMED CONSENT 210 (2014). Arguably, however, "consultation" here implies an international standard that can be linked to important instruments. Specifically, the International Labour Organization's Convention (No. 169) concerning Indigenous and Tribal Peoples in Independent Countries art. 6, June 27, 1989, 1650 U.N.T.S. 383, embodies the international legal duty to carry out consultations "whenever consideration is being given to legislative or administrative measures which may affect [Indigenous peoples] directly."

[129] Sarfaty, *supra* note 125, at 1801.

[130] Bradlow, *supra* note 126, at 55.

[131] See generally *The Equator Principles*, EQUATOR PRINCIPLES, http://www.equator-principles .com/about. See also, Bank of America Corporation Environmental and Social Risk Policy Framework Apr. 2019 https://about.bankofamerica.com/assets/pdf/Environmental-and-Social-Risk-Policy-Framework.pdf.

Adopted by ninety-four private financial institutions in thirty-seven countries, the Equator Principles are voluntary but may affect the majority of international project finance debt within developed and emerging markets.[132]

* * *

In short, international financial institutions, primarily led by the WBG, have sought to finance development projects in a more sustainable, appropriate and culturally sensitive manner. Protections outlined in their operational policies are incorporated by reference as binding obligations in lending agreements and, overall, seek to ensure the participation of indigenous communities in the planning process and to prevent adverse impacts on tribes. The enforcement is imperfect as it takes place within the accountability and justice systems of the financial institutions themselves. But safeguards have the potential to establish international norms regarding foreseeable harm, and influence the actions of governments and private lenders. Nevertheless, competition among financial institutions might fragment the quality of protections established by the standards or their application. Finally, without the inclusion by governments of Indigenous peoples in social protection and development priorities, IFIs have limited capacity to change the reality of Indigenous peoples. When governments take action as a response to the leverage exercised by international development banks:

> [t]he extent to which social protection programmes benefit Indigenous peoples and ethnic minorities depends on whether they address the needs of and challenges faced by these groups. Involving their representatives in the design and implementation of programmes is one way of ensuring that they better address the needs of Indigenous peoples and ethnic minorities and reflect the reality in which they live.[133]

---

[132] *Id.* Like the safeguards put in place by IFIs, the Equator Principles require recipients of loans to conduct social impact assessments, obtain the free, prior and informed consent of any affected Indigenous peoples, and develop plans to mitigate any adverse impacts. Nonetheless, as adoption of the Equator Principles is entirely voluntary, questions of their efficacy are not unreasonable. The Principles themselves state that they "do not create any rights in, or liability to, any person, public or private." *Id.* at 11.

[133] UNDESA PROMOTING INCLUSION THROUGH SOCIAL PROTECTION: REPORT ON THE WORLD SOCIAL SITUATION 2018 (New York: United Nations, 2018) 108, visit https://www.un.org/development/desa/dspd/wp-content/uploads/sites/22/2018/07/1-1.pdf.

3.2.3 *Trade*

The impact of trade agreements on indigenous communities has been widely documented.[134] Yet, express protections for Indigenous peoples are only just emerging within these instruments.[135] Taubman lists at least thirty-three trade treaties with formal recognition of Indigenous peoples rights or other protections, including specific benefits, exceptions, the right to free, prior and informed consultation and IP protections.[136] In addition, as human rights, indigenous rights may be explicitly safeguarded under broader human rights protections or general exceptions (a topic I address elsewhere in this book). Yet, according to Cambridge University Professor, Lorand Bartels, "it is not always clear that the general exceptions tend to permit a party to impose trade restrictions in order to safeguard human rights in the other country: indeed, a specific exception to this effect . . . proves the rule." Notably, there is also an increasing overlap between indigenous rights provisions and environmental protection, especially in the context of trans-boundary pollution, which may

---

[134] Consider the analysis of the European Commission of the EU & Colombia & Peru FTA "In July 2012, the Commission published the assessment of the economic impact of the trade agreement between the EU and Colombia and Peru. According to the document, the agreement should have a positive impact on the gross domestic product (GDP) of both partner economies; for Colombia GDP growth of around 0.4% (~ €500 million) was estimated and for Peru GDP growth of between 0.2% and 0.25% (~ €200 million). The estimated gains to the EU were small (€2.3 billion, less than 0.05 % of GDP). The effect of bilateral trade was estimated as positive: the EU's exports to Colombia and Peru would increase by 63% (€2.5 billion) and 48% (€2 billion) respectively; the EU's imports from Colombia would increase by 11% (€390 million) and from Peru by 15% (€340 million)." This analysis also includes a reference to Saura's (2013), "which analysed the negotiation process and warned of negative effects on food, health, water, sanitation and land that would be felt most severely by vulnerable groups, including informal workers, farmers, Afro-Colombians, Indigenous people and women. Some of these impacts had already been demonstrated in the context of the GSP+ trade regime, which also included safeguards for rights and freedoms. Now that the Trade Agreement is in place, there do not seem to be many promising signs of change, according to the author."

[135] See generally Wai, *supra* note 1, at 45 (2003) (discussing the increase of human rights concerns in international trade regulation).

[136] EU & Colombia & Peru; Peru & Republic of Korea; Colombia & Republic of Korea; EU & CARIFORUM States; China & Costa Rica; EFTA & Colombia; EFTA & Peru; Nicaragua & Taiwan; Peru & China; Guatemala & Taiwan; Panama & Taiwan; Switzerland & China; China & Republic of Korea; Costa Rica & Singapore; New Zealand & Malaysia; EU & Ukraine; Thailand & New Zealand; EU & Republic of Korea; Australia & China; Hong Kong China & New Zealand; Republic of Korea & New Zealand; ASEAN & Australia & New Zealand; New Zealand & Taiwan; Japan & Thailand; Canada & Panama; Canada & Peru; Economic Cooperation Organization ("ECO"); U.S. & Colombia; U.S. & Peru; Canada & Colombia; and the TransPacific Strategic Economic Partnership.

be capaciously deployed in transnational trade matters.[137] The *Aerial Spraying Case*, a case initiated by Ecuador before the ICJ illustrates this point. Ecuador filed the case in 2007 following alleged cross-border spraying of herbicides by Colombia aircraft during anti-narcotic operations. Ecuador argued, *inter alia*, that the resulting pollution violated the human rights of Indigenous people in Ecuador whose health, crops and livestock had suffered.[138]

These protections thus only imperfectly advance the interest of Indigenous peoples. There are usually no specific trade benefits provided to indigenous groups – although some governments have included specific benefits such as market access for indigenous goods (the textiles chapter of the USMCA provides for duty-free treatment of some indigenous goods).[139] Provisions like these (granting special benefits to vulnerable populations) tend to be consistent with the goals and the interpretation of trade treaties and have been welcomed by specialists in many contexts, including indigenous rights.[140] Governments have also relied on broader legal basis for temporal benefits for indigenous groups.[141] Nevertheless, most specific protections in current treaty practice usually entail reservations and exceptions to, or carve-outs and exemptions from, obligations that restrict states from granting advantages – such as an exclusive or preferential treatment – to indigenous communities, their products or production methods. An interesting example of a general application is the broad *Māori exception* included in the CP-TPP, and replicated in other trade deals of New Zealand. These carve-outs protect against the narrowing of the group's advantages secured under the Treaty of Waitangi, permits more favorable treatment to the Maori People and

---

[137] Alan Boyle, *Human Rights and the Environment: Where Next* 23 Eur. J. Int. Law, 613–42 (2012), visit https://academic.oup.com/ejil/article/23/3/613/399894. See also generally Jean-Frédéric Morin et al., Mapping the Trade and Environment Nexus: Insights from a New Data Set Global Environmental Politics 18:1, (Feb. 2018), https://www.chaire-epi.ulaval.ca/sites/chaire-epi.ulaval.ca/files/publications/trend_2.pdf. I thank Dr. D Azaria for helpful comment about this topic.

[138] See *Aerial Herbicide Spraying (Ecuador v. Colombia)*, https://www.icj-cij.org/en/case/138.

[139] See USMCA, art. 6.2, https://ustr.gov/sites/default/files/files/agreements/FTA/USMCA/Text/06_Textiles_and_Apparel.pdf.

[140] See e.g., Charles M. Gastle, Shadows of a Talking Circle: Aboriginal Advocacy Before International Institutions and Tribunals 5 (2002) (explaining that "nations jealously guard their sovereignty and the recognition of aboriginal groups").

[141] In 2006 the U.S. government allowed the Navajo Nation to sell Cuba beans, corn, wheat and other products. The United States relied on exceptions to the trade embargo for agricultural goods paid for in cash for this benefit, https://www.npr.org/templates/story/story.php?storyId=5701604.

guarantee the substantive rights recognized under other legal instruments.[142] The exception reads as follows:

Article 29.6: Treaty of Waitangi

1   Provided that such measures are not used as a means of arbitrary or unjustified discrimination against persons of the other Parties or as a disguised restriction on trade in goods, trade in services and investment, nothing in this Agreement shall preclude the adoption by New Zealand of measures it deems necessary to accord more favorable treatment to Maori in respect of matters covered by this Agreement, including in fulfillment of its obligations under the Treaty of Waitangi.

2   The Parties agree that the interpretation of the Treaty of Waitangi, including as to the nature of the rights and obligations arising under it, shall not be subject to the dispute settlement provisions of this Agreement. Chapter 28 (Dispute Settlement) shall otherwise apply to this Article. A panel established under Article 28.7 (Establishment of a Panel) may be requested to determine only whether any measure referred to in paragraph 1 is inconsistent with a Party's rights under this Agreement.

An example of a narrower, but general exception can be found in the recently signed USMCA. Despite an ambitious attempt by the Government of Canada to include important innovations,[143] the final text follows the trend in treaty practice. Canada's proposal for a progressive treaty included a chapter recognizing rights and special benefits due to tribes. At the end, the USMCA included the following exception:

Article 32.5: Indigenous Peoples Rights

Provided that such measures are not used as a means of arbitrary or unjustified discrimination against persons of the other Parties or as a disguised restriction on trade in goods, services, and investment, this Agreement does not preclude a Party from adopting or maintaining a measure it deems necessary to fulfill its legal obligations to Indigenous peoples.

---

[142] Comprehensive and Progressive Agreement for Trans-Pacific Partnership art. 29.6, Mar. 8, 2018, https://www.mfat.govt.nz/assets/Trans-Pacific-Partnership/Text/29.-Exceptions-and-General-Provisions.pdf [hereinafter CP-TPP] (protections concerning the Maori people and the Treaty of Waitangi).

[143] Canada's initial proposal included an indigenous chapter to address issues such as protection of cultural rights, special incentives in specific sectors and for investment, see, *Canada Wants a New NAFTA to Include Gender and Indigenous Rights*, N.Y. TIMES, Aug. 14, 2017.

One shortcoming of this approach is that exceptions tend to have narrower application, and need to be asserted by the party relying on that provision. Hence, many authors have suggested that it could be useful to include state obligations and a broader human rights clause that specifically authorizes a party to comply with – or facilitate compliance with – human rights treaties (including indigenous rights) to avoid having to justify the applicability of an exception in a particular case. Nonetheless, some argue that indigenous and human rights issues should not be addressed through a global trading system and doubt that the system even has the institutional capacity to address these complexities.[144] Instead, they argue for stronger enforcement alternatives in regional institutions that have the appropriate knowledge, resources and capacity to address adequately social issues – for instance, the Inter-American Court of Human Rights (IACtHR) or the International Labour Organization.[145] Several cases before the IACtHR have shown the potential of regional institutions to address potential violations of indigenous rights when decisions over economic issues are made – a topic that I address shortly.[146]

While debate over the convenience of including provisions like this in trade agreements will continue, it is clear that the time has arrived for linking trade and Indigenous peoples. If the aspiration is to have truly "progressive" agreements that address the historical injustice, material inequality and precarious conditions of indigenous groups, the debate has to move beyond the exceptional treatment and also beyond the formal recognition of state obligations toward Indigenous peoples in the treaty text. It *must* address ways of empowering indigenous interests, including by establishing mechanisms to foster economic policies that transfer wealth. One potential avenue is by recognizing market access for goods and services relevant for Indigenous peoples or by limiting valid subsidies on the condition of the recipient status, including for vulnerable and marginalized communities. This is of course controversial and a question of a political nature that involves not only the current political economy of the systems of production, distribution and consumption, but

---

[144] Mike Moore, A World without Walls: Freedom, Development, Free Trade and Global Governance 101 (2003).

[145] James L. Cavallaro & Jaime O'Connell, *When Prosecution Is Not Enough: How the International Criminal Court Can Prevent Atrocity and Advance Accountability by Emulating Regional Human Rights Institutions*, 45 Yale J. Int'l L. 1 (2020).

[146] *Comunidades Indígenas Miembros de la Asociación Lhaka Honhat (Nuestra Tierra) v. Argentina*, Inter-Am. Ct. H.R. (Feb 6, 2020) [hereinafter IACtHR]. (In its judgment, the Court determined that the State violated the right to community property, by not providing legal security to it and allowing the presence of "creole," nonindigenous, residents in the territory. It also concluded that Argentina does not have adequate regulations to guarantee sufficiently the community property right).

more generally to reconceptualize metrics of success of trade agreements based on the needs of vulnerable populations. This is not to say that these two conversations can be linked – perhaps in some instances more effectively – outside of trade institutions. But as long as the venue is trade institutions the conversation will be *trade and*, and not *Indigenous peoples and*.

Moreover, multilateral organizations outside the domain of economic issues have avoided addressing the issue. One noteworthy example of this linkage between *trade and indigenous concerns* outside of trade institutions is the 2005 UNESCO Convention, which mandates a broad list of trade-related measures to protect indigenous cultural heritage, including cultural goods and services.[147] This is a rather narrow topic, with a complicated history. The scope includes "policies and measures adopted by the [now 145 treaty] Parties related to the protection and promotion of the diversity of cultural expressions." In its more relevant section, Article 7 of the treaty mandates actions to promote cultural expressions. It states that:

1   Parties shall endeavour to create in their territory an environment which encourages:
    (a) to create, produce, disseminate, distribute and have access to their own cultural expressions, paying due attention to the special circumstances and needs of women as well as various social groups, including persons belonging to minorities and Indigenous peoples;
    (b) to have access to diverse cultural expressions from within their territory as well as from other countries of the world.
2   Parties shall also endeavour to recognize the important contribution of artists, others involved in the creative process, cultural communities, and organizations that support their work, and their central role in nurturing the diversity of cultural expressions.

It is unclear – especially in this day and age – whether international organizations outside of the trade realm like UNESCO can address this important linkage in a more effective way for Indigenous peoples' interests. But it is also unclear whether organizations like the WTO, which tends to be a forum for trade negotiations for strong and vested economic interests can really deal with questions of economic empowerment of vulnerable populations and social

---

[147] 2005 Convention, *supra* note 99. For a more detailed discussion on trade and cultural heritage, see generally T. Voon, *Substantive WTO Law and the Convention on the Diversity of Cultural Expression*, in THE UNESCO CONVENTION ON THE DIVERSITY OF CULTURAL EXPRESSIONS: A TALE OF FRAGMENTATION IN INTERNATIONAL LAW 273 (Toshiyuki Kono & Steven Van Uytsel eds., 2012).

justice, especially when these institutions have limited context of these issues. However, many scholars view the international trading system as compatible with and necessary for the protection of human rights, including indigenous rights. For example, the former Dean of Yale Law School Harold Koh notes that WTO treaties do not generally conflict with obligations enumerated in other instruments and that trade adjudicators have begun to display more tolerance for regulations designed to address the goals of human rights obligations that have "discriminatory" or "trade-restrictive" effects.[148] In particular, governments can rely on exceptions designed to protect specified objectives, such as the protection of human health, life and public morals, or to secure compliance with laws or regulations to defend policies of that nature.[149] For example, the Appellate Body ("AB") of the WTO recently held that key provisions can be used to excuse a treaty breach when trade restrictive measures are adopted to protect the interests of indigenous groups.[150] As a result, advocates for Indigenous peoples have begun to push for further acknowledgment of their interests within the trading system.[151] Specifically, the recognition of the duty to consult with Indigenous peoples when a potential agreement could affect those peoples is a priority.[152] Such recognition has also begun to take place in certain domestic courts and other bodies; notably, the Inter-American Commission of Human Rights has demanded indigenous consultation prior to ratifications of FTAs and the Costa Rican Constitutional Court struck down draft legislation aimed at implementing the Central America Free Trade Agreement because the government failed to consult with Indigenous peoples beforehand.[153]

---

[148] Harold Hongju Koh, *Global Tobacco Control as a Health and Human Rights Imperative*, 57 Harv. Int'l L.J. 433, 440–41 (2016).

[149] General Agreement on Trade in Services art. XIV, Apr. 15, 1994, Marrakesh Agreement Establishing the World Trade Organization, Annex 1B, 1869 U.N.T.S. 183, 33 I.L.M. 1167 (1994) [hereinafter GATS]; The General Agreement on Tariffs and Trade art. XX, Oct. 30, 1947, 61 Stat. A-11, 55 U.N.T.S. 194 [hereinafter GATT]. For the reliance on the exceptions, Members must satisfy the requirements that the measures at issue are "not applied in a manner which would constitute a means of arbitrary or unjustifiable discrimination . . . or a disguised restriction on international trade." *Id.*

[150] Appellate Body Report, *European Communities – Measures Prohibiting the Importation and Marketing of Seal Products*, ¶ 5.338, WTO Doc. WT/DS400/AB/R & WT/DS401/AB/R (May 22, 2014).

[151] *See IACHR: Demands on Indigenous Consultation to Ratify Free Trade Agreements*, IWGIA (Dec. 15, 2016), [hereinafter Demands on Indigenous Consultation].

[152] *Id.*

[153] Int'l Ctr. for Trade & Sustainable Dev., Costa Rica's Long Road to CAFTA, Bridges (Nov. 6, 2008), http://www.ictsd.org/bridges-news/bridges/news/costa-rica's-long-road-to-cafta.

One thing is clear: international trade features few explicit protections of Indigenous peoples. Those that do exist are almost always in the form of reservations, exceptions or carve-outs that allow discriminatory (*de jure* or *de facto*) or trade restrictive measures to be adopted in order for a state to comply with human rights obligations or better to accommodate the interests and practices of Indigenous peoples. The limited reliance on such legal provisions to build more robust protections may be explained by a state's tendency to favor economic interests over indigenous rights. And, even when trade agreements provide sufficient flexibility to accommodate indigenous rights – an issue that I discuss in the next section – indigenous groups often lack mechanisms to influence domestic trade policy or the outcomes of proceedings before dispute settlement bodies like the WTO-DSU.[154]

3.2.4 *Investment*

Indigenous peoples are susceptible to the effects of treaties that attempt to encourage FDI by granting special rights to foreign investors (and an arbitration process outside normal, national courts to enforce such rights).[155] However, according to the Special Rapporteur on the Rights of Indigenous peoples even in the absence of investment treaties "foreign and domestic investment has a serious impact on Indigenous peoples' rights."[156] Particularly impactful are investments in oil, coal, gas and minerals extraction that affect traditional territories, but also tend to lead to more long-term impacts on the well-being of indigenous communities.[157] These sectors,

---

[154] See Soopramanien, *supra* note 40, at 242.

[155] Victoria Tauli-Corpuz (Special Rapporteur of the Human Rights Council), *Report of the Special Rapporteur on the Rights of Indigenous Peoples – International Investment Agreements, Including Bilateral Investment Treaties and Investment Chapters of Free Trade Agreements*, ¶¶ 31–40, U.N. Doc. A/HRC/33/42 (Aug. 11, 2016). Valentina S. Vadi, *When Cultures Collide: Foreign Direct Investment, Natural Resources, and Indigenous Heritage in International Investment Law*, 42 COLUM. HUM. RTS. L. REV. 797, 836 (2011). See also, J. Levine, *The Interaction of International Investment Arbitration and the Rights of Indigenous Peoples*, in BAETENS, THE INTERACTION OF INTERNATIONAL INVESTMENT LAW WITH OTHER FIELDS OF INTERNATIONAL LAW (n 3); M. Krepchev, *The Problem of Accommodating Indigenous Land Rights in International Investment Law*, 6 JIDS 42 (2015).

[156] *Id.* Victoria Tauli-Corpuz ¶ 78.

[157] *See* James Anaya (Special Rapporteur on the Rights of Indigenous Peoples), *Extractive Industries Operating Within or Near Indigenous Territories*, ¶¶ 30–55, U.N. Doc. A/HRC/18/35 (July 11, 2011). (According to the Special Rapporteur: "the business model that still prevails in most places for the extraction of natural resources within indigenous territories is not one that is fully conducive to the fulfillment of indigenous peoples' rights, particularly their self-determination, proprietary and cultural rights in relation to the affected lands and resources . . . [Also] the prevailing model of resource extraction is one in which an outside company, with

which often follow a similar business model, also are primary users and beneficiaries of the international investment regime to insulate investments from "political risk".[158]

How does the international investment law system – one that empowers foreign investors – affect Indigenous peoples? The simple answer is: mostly indirectly. For many commentators, the main problem with the current system of international investment law is its enforcement system – a mechanism that gives foreign investors a private right of action to make governments accountable for their legal or regulatory measures based on vague standards of conduct. In turn, this system encourages riskier investments or more aggressive behavior by investors, who can demand from states to restrain its regulatory powers or else sue them before an international tribunal. The main problem here is that the *ad hoc* tribunals of party-appointed arbitrators resolve one-off disputes between the investor and the State, even though the disputes might involve public law or complex policy issues and directly affect local communities.[159] Moreover, given the potential for large damage awards, the threat of litigation can chill regulation or force the State to side with already empowered foreign interest in detriment of other state constituencies.[160]

backing by the State, controls and profits from the extractive operation, with the affected Indigenous peoples at best being offered benefits in the form of jobs or community development projects that typically pale in economic value in comparison to profits gained by the corporation."). In recent years, models of contractual arrangement have led to the incorporation of environmental and social controls – including indigenous rights – into agreements between mining companies and governments. See, e.g., Int'l Inst. for Sustainable Dev., *The IBA's Model Mining Development Agreement: A New Paradigm for Natural Resource Projects*, INVEST. TREATY NEWS, Sept. 2010, at 7, http://www.iisd.org/itn/wp-content/uploads/2010/09/IISDITNnewsletter_ SEPTWEB.pdf.

[158] JONATHAN BONNITCHA, LAUGE POULSEN & MICHAEL WAIBEL, THE POLITICAL ECONOMY OF THE INVESTMENT TREATY REGIME (Oxford: Oxford University Press, 2017). Dupont, Cédric, Thomas Schultz, Melanie Wahl & Merih Angin, *Types of Political Risk Leading to Investment Arbitrations in the Oil & Gas Sector*, 8 JWELB, 337–61 (2015).

[159] Gus Van Harten & Martin Loughlin, *Investment Treaty Arbitration as a Species of Global Administrative Law*, 17 EUR. J. INT'L L. 121, 131–33 (2006); Anthea Roberts, *Clash of Paradigms: Actors and Analogies Shaping the Investment Treaty System*, 107 AJIL 45, 92 (2013) (discussing criticism of ISDS proposing a new theoretical framework to explain the investment treaty system). The community interest has to be represented by the state, unless a third party can bring arguments (although generally not a claim) before the tribunal. See infra.

[160] Kyla Tienhaara, *Regulatory Chill and the Threat of Arbitration: A View from Political Science*, in EVOLUTION IN INVESTMENT TREATY LAW AND ARBITRATION 606, 606 (Chester Brown & Kate Miles eds., 2011) (arguing that regulatory chill is an important problem "inadequately addressed and often prematurely dismissed by legal scholars"). It is also argued that "the tribunals interpret vague treaty rules—such as provisions demanding 'fair and equitable treatment' and prohibitions against 'measures tantamount to expropriation.' The system lacks

As is the case with trade regimes, specific protections for Indigenous peoples in investment treaties are rare and, when they *do* exist, relatively weak – especially when compared with the protections against excessive state behavior that foreign investors enjoy through BITs or FTAs. One example of such indigenous protections is the investment chapter of NAFTA, in which Canada and the United States obtained exemptions from investment obligations in order to adopt or maintain any measure denying investors rights or preferences provided to Indigenous peoples.[161] Specifically, exemptions of this nature aim at reinforcing state powers to protect indigenous land and natural resources from exploitation, competition or liberalization.[162]

Indigenous peoples also receive some protection in BITs that occasionally impose more general obligations to protect human rights. For instance, the 2016 Morocco-Nigeria BIT imposes obligations to "ensure that their laws, policies and actions are consistent with the international human rights agreements" and imposes obligations on investors not to "manage or operate the investments in a manner that circumvents international ... human rights obligations."[163] While there are other notable exceptions to the general

---

an appeal process, other than a narrow annulment proceeding that has been routinely criticized. Conflicting decisions, sometimes involving the same facts, raise rule-of-law and coherence concerns. Because the arbitrators are appointed on an *ad hoc* basis as opposed to a fixed term and are allowed to represent clients in other arbitrations (conduct known as 'double hatting'), they face incentives to decide cases in a manner that favors the party that appointed them and to assure a flow of future cases, sparking challenges to their independence and impartiality.") *See* Sergio Puig & Gregory Shaffer, *Imperfect Alternatives: Institutional Choice and the Reform of Investment Law*, 112 AM. J. INT'L L. 361 (2018).

[161] North American Free Trade Agreement, Can.-Mex.-U.S., art. 1102, Dec. 17, 1992, 32 I.L.M. 612, 641 (1993) ("Canada reserves the right to adopt or maintain any measure denying investors of another Party and their investments, or service providers of another Party, any rights or preferences provided to aboriginal peoples") (hereinafter NAFTA Annex II); *id.* (including in the list of exceptions for the United States, similar exceptions also apply to "socially or economically disadvantaged minorities"). Provisions similar to these protections have been reported in the USMCA, *supra* note 9. Other protections can be found in CETA. This pending treaty has a complete carve-out against "any measure adopted or maintained with respect to Aboriginal peoples, nor to set aside for aboriginal businesses; existing aboriginal or treaty rights of any of the Aboriginal peoples of Canada protected by section 35 of the Constitution Act, 1982."

[162] For other approaches, see e.g. Lise Johnson, Lisa Sachs & Jesse Coleman, *International Investment Agreements, 2014: A Review of Trends and New Approaches*, in Andrea K. Bjorklund (ed.), YEARBOOK ON INTERNATIONAL INVESTMENT LAW & POLICY 2014–2015 (Oxford University Press 2016), at 50–60.

[163] Reciprocal Investment Promotion and Protection Agreement between the Government of the Kingdom of Morocco and the Government of the Federal Republic of Nigeria, Morocco-Nigeria, arts. 15 & 18, Mar. 12, 2016, http://investmentpolicyhub.unctad.org/Download/TreatyFile/5409. Also, India's Model Bilateral Investment Treaty (December 2015) also provides that "[a]n investor may not submit a claim to arbitration under this Chapter if the

trend,[164] compliance with indigenous rights (or human rights for that matter) often is not explicitly referred to as a cause to justify conduct inconsistent with investment arrangements.[165] Some argue that this is due to the desire by states to encourage investment from MNCs and that explicit exceptions might discourage investment.[166] Empirical evidence, however, seems to run counter to the hypothetical correlation that less legal protections for vulnerable groups entails higher levels of investment.[167]

The lack of stronger language to protect the interests of Indigenous peoples might also have something to do with the structure of investment law (and its enforcement system) as a regime designed to protect MNCs. Because investment law involves assessing how the state deals with business actors, some scholars argue that putting human rights requirements expressly in investment treaties is unnecessary. According to this argument, states already possess the power to protect human rights against private (mis)conduct within their own respective domestic legal frameworks.[168]

---

investment has been made through fraudulent misrepresentation, concealment, corruption, money laundering or conduct amounting to an abuse of process or similar illegal mechanisms." India Model Bilateral Investment Treaty, art. 13.4.

[164] See, e.g., UNCTAD, Norway Model Bilateral Investment Treaty art. 6 (2015), http://investmentpolicyhub.unctad.org/Download/TreatyFile/3350 ("Paragraphs 1 to 6 of this Article do not in any circumstances apply to a measure or a series of measures, other than nationalizing or expropriating, by a Party that are designed and applied to safeguard public interests, such as measures to meet … human rights … concerns").

[165] See Tauli-Corpuz, *supra* note 155 at 225 ¶ 71.

[166] *The Double Life of International Law: Indigenous Peoples and Extractive Industries*, 129 Harv. L. Rev. 1755, 1764 (2016).

[167] See, e.g., Robert J. Flanagan, *Labor Standards and International Competitive Advantage*, in International Labor Standards: Globalization, Trade, and Public Policy 15, 29–31 (Robert J. Flanagan & William B. Gould IV eds., 2003).

[168] See generally Charles N. Brower & Sadie Blanchard, *What's in a Meme? The Truth about Investor-State Arbitration: Why It Need Not, and Must Not, Be Repossessed by States*, 52 Colum. J. Transnat'l L. 689 (2014). According to some views, in case of conflict international law recognizes the primacy of human rights over investor protection, see, Sawhoyamaxa, Indigenous Community v. Paraguay, Merits, Reparations, and Costs, Judgment, Inter-Am. Ct. H.R. (ser. C) No. 146, ¶ 128. (Mar. 29, 2006). See also Xákmok Kásek Indigenous Community. v. Paraguay, Merits, Reparations, and Costs, Judgment, Inter-Am. Ct. H.R. (ser. C) No. 214, ¶ 109 (Aug. 24, 2010). Certainly, some investment treaties include WTO-like expectation to investment obligations. See, for instance, the Canada-Colombia Free Trade Agreement states that: "For the purposes of Chapter Eight (Investment), subject to the requirement that such measures are not applied in a manner that constitute arbitrary or unjustifiable discrimination between investment or between investors, or a disguised restriction on international trade or investment, nothing in this Agreement shall be construed to prevent a Party from adopting or enforcing measures necessary:

To protect human, animal or plant life or health, which the Parties understand to include environmental measures necessary to protect human, animal or plant life and health;

And other international institutions might have competing authority (e.g., the African Court on Human and Peoples' Rights) over state actions or omissions relating to the investment projects that violate or that are implicated in the affectation of indigenous rights.[169] This argument also suggests that the obligations *vis-à-vis* the investor shall not be read by interpretative bodies, *prima facie*, in an inconsistent manner with other protections afforded under human rights obligations (harmonization). Moreover, even if it were the case that inconsistency exists, states have the right or even the duty to implement measures designed to protect human rights (prioritization);[170] the state simply has to pay compensation to any investor whose investment has been *unduly* and, perhaps, disproportionally affected when it does so. Therefore, if states were to add justificatory exceptions (like in international trade), it would signal that investment obligations might not be easily reconcilable with human rights, or that investment tribunals should not balance different state interests when interpreting treaty obligations. This type of tension is common in the interpretation of economic arrangements.

Another controversial question in the investment law system, which only indirectly involves Indigenous peoples, concerns whether human rights violations in which a foreign investor is implicated limit their rights under investment treaties.[171] Depending on the language of the treaty, such action may be invoked by the host state under the compliance-with-the-law requirement to avoid responsibility or lead to an element of contributory fault, therefore affecting the amount due as a result of treaty violations.[172]

    To ensure compliance with laws and regulations that are not inconsistent with this Agreement; or

    For the conservation of living or non-living exhaustible natural resources.

[169] In a case before the IACtHR, the judges faced the question of interpreting a BIT in the light of indigenous rights commitments. Sawhoyamaxa Indigenous Community v Paraguay, Inter-American Court of Human Rights, Judgment of 29 March 2006. See for a discussion P. Nikken, *Balancing of Human Rights and Investment Law in the Inter-American System of Human Rights*, in DUPUY, FRANCIONI AND PETERSMANN, HUMAN RIGHTS IN INTERNATIONAL INVESTMENT LAW (n 3).

[170] Johannes Hendrik Fahner & Matthew Happold, 68 ICLQ 741–59 (2019). Sawhoyamaxa Indigenous Community v Paraguay, Inter-American Court of Human Rights, Judgment of 29 March 2006.

[171] P. Dumberry & G. Dumas-Aubin, *When and How Allegations of Human Rights Violations Can Be Raised in Investor-State Arbitration*, JWIT 349 (2012).

[172] Phoenix Action Ltd v. Czech Republic, ICSID ARB/06/5, Award of 15 Apr. 2009, para 78. Copper Mesa Mining Corp v. Ecuador, PCA 2012–2, Award of Mar. 15, 2016, para 6.99, 6.102.

Beyond these (and perhaps other) doctrinal debates, there are important legal and practical consequences of not including specific exception or carve-out language.[173] Nevertheless, there is some value in this approach. For one, specific protections are already established in other human rights treaties that regulate the relationship between Indigenous peoples and the state, and provide for the potential responsibility of the latter (although, as I will explain, not that of the investor).[174] Moreover, after all, when interpreting *all* economic treaties, international adjudicators are required to adhere to the Vienna Convention on the Law of Treaties, which provides that other applicable rules of international law be considered.[175] Through this rule of interpretation, the protections established elsewhere, in other sources of legal authority, have some bearing in the interpretation of the relationship between the investor (or right holder) and the state regulated by the BIT – either as a relevant context (emerging as a duty of care) or as a rule between the treaty parties.[176] Moreover, if a breach of indigenous rights results from the implementation of, or compliance with, an investment treaty, the rules on state responsibility demand mitigation efforts, and domestic or human rights law might provide a cause of action for reparation (against the State).[177] As explained, for the investor, it might result in

---

[173] Cf. Pamela B. Gann, *The U.S. Bilateral Investment Treaty Program*, 21 STAN. J. INT'L L. 373, 390 (1985) (noting that incorporating human rights protections into investment treaty "may give those rules and principles greater effectiveness ... through the dispute settlement provisions").

[174] See, e.g., Mayagna (Sumo) Awas Tingni Community v. Nicaragua, Merits, Reparations and Costs, Judgment, Inter-Am. Ct. H.R. (ser. C) No. 79, ¶ 153 (Aug. 31, 2001) (holding that in granting a concession to two foreign companies to log land claimed by the indigenous Awas Tingni group, Nicaragua had violated the American Convention on Human Rights by infringing upon the Awas Tingni Community's right to "the use and enjoyment of their property"); Saramaka People v. Suriname, Preliminary Objections, Merits, Reparations, and Costs, Judgment, Inter-Am. Ct. H.R. (ser. C) No. 172, ¶¶ 12, 142 (Nov. 28, 2007) (condemning the environmental degradation caused by foreign companies within territory traditionally owned by the Saramaka community); Kichwa Indigenous People of Sarayaku v. Ecuador, Merits and Reparations, Judgment, Inter-Am. Ct. H.R. (ser. C) No. 245, ¶¶ 75, 147, 305 (June 27, 2012) (the Court ruled that the failure to consult the Indigenous peoples and obtain their free, prior and informed consent, and the use of force by the State, had put the Indigenous peoples' survival at risk); Kaliña and Lokono Peoples v. Suriname, Merits, Reparations and Costs, Judgment, Inter-Am. Ct. H.R. (ser. C) No. 309, ¶¶ 200–1 (Nov. 25, 2015).

[175] Vienna Convention on the Law of Treaties, art. 31(3)(c), May 23, 1969, 8 I.L.M. 679, 1155 U.N.T.S. 331; see also Valentina S. Vadi, *When Cultures Collide: Foreign Direct Investment, Natural Resources, and Indigenous Heritage in International Investment Law*, 42 COLUM. HUM. RTS. L. REV. 797, 866 (2011).

[176] Hendrik Fahner & Matthew Happold *supra* note 170.

[177] See Int'l Law Comm'n, Rep. on the Work of Its Fifty-Third Session, U.N. Doc. A/56/10, at 43–50 (2001).

"contributory responsibility, by reason of its acts and omissions," potentially affecting any compensation due.[178]

Indubitably, many arbitrators in investor–state arbitration, currently the preferred mechanism to enforce rights conferred upon investors, often lack experience in human rights law.[179] This might explain why some tribunals seem reluctant to give broader consideration to these elements (effectively reducing the scope of indigenous rights) and can make the aforementioned analysis seem a little naive.[180] Moreover, for the most part, arbitrators lack jurisdiction to find business actors in breach of international law. For these reasons, many scholars argue that BITs should include explicit language that in conflicts regarding human rights and investment, certain human rights treaties shall prevail.[181] Others more forcefully argue for the reform of investment treaty regime.[182]

In response to these (and other) critiques, states and commentators have proposed a range of institutional reforms to eliminate or radically to transform ISDS.[183] Prominently, the EU has promoted a multilateral investment court system where private investors retain standing to file claims directly against states. However, through a network of treaties the EU will rely on a tribunal of first instance and an appellate body, with the judges having fixed terms, receiving a regular salary and being selected on a random basis from a roster designated by states.[184] The EU has already concluded agreements containing such a system – designed for bilateral relations, but including flexibilities for

---

[178] Bear Creek Mining Corporation v. Republic of Peru, ICSID Case No. ARB/14/21, Partial Dissenting Opinion, ¶¶ 3–4 (Nov. 30, 2017). (Sands also suggests that at the very least the company had an obligation to obtain "social license").

[179] Megan Wells Sheffer, *Bilateral Investment Treaties: A Friend or Foe to Human Rights?* 39 DENVER J. INT'L L. & POL'Y 483, 495–96 (2011).

[180] *Id.* For example, in Bernhard von Pezold and Others v. Republic of Zimbabwe, ICSID Case No. ARB/10/15, Procedural Order No. 2, ¶ 60 (June 26, 2012), the Tribunal composed by Mr. L. Yves Fortier, Professor David A. R. Williams and Professor An Chen decided that "the putative rights of the indigenous communities as 'Indigenous peoples' under international human rights law, [was] a matter outside of the scope of the dispute." It also determined that it was up to the Tribunal to "decide whether the indigenous communities constitute 'Indigenous peoples' for the purposes of grounding any rights under international human rights law." *Id.*

[181] See Barnali Choudhury, *Exception Provisions as a Gateway to Incorporating Human Rights Issues into International Investment Agreements*, 49 COLUM. J. TRANSNAT'L L. 670, 688, 711 (2011).

[182] See generally Lorenzo Cotula, *Rethinking Investment Treaties to Advance Human Rights*, INTERNATIONAL INSTITUTE FOR ENVIRONMENT AND DEVELOPMENT (2016).

[183] Roberts, *supra* note 159, at M-6-9. See also, Puig & Sheffer *supra* note 160.

[184] European Commission, *Investment in TTIP and Beyond – The Path for Reform, Enhancing the Right to Regulate and Moving from Current ad hoc Arbitration towards an Investment Court*, 11 (May 2015), http://trade.ec.europa.eu/doclib/docs/2015/may/tradoc_153408.PDF (concluding

multilateralization – with Canada, Singapore, Vietnam and Mexico, and indications that more agreements with these features will follow.[185] Notably, and perhaps more relevant for Indigenous peoples, the investment court system plans to make raising counter-claims against the investor an easier task. If created, the court will make clear that counter-claims are possible if the conduct of the investor could be raised by the state or by a right holder in the case of a violation of a commitment. These could be useful innovations (or clarifications); as it currently exists ISDS fails appropriately to balance competing interests, in part because of the inability of states and other stakeholders to raise effective claims and counter-claims against investors.

* * *

A few provisions exist within international economic arrangements for the protection of Indigenous peoples, but they are often under-enforced, weak or hamstrung by other forces or competing interests. Protections tend to be stronger in IP, which creates *sui generis* rights, and finance, which relies on safeguards directly incorporated in loan agreements. Protections in international trade and investment tend to be weaker. The first regulates the relationship between distinct legal obligations through reservations, carve-outs or exceptions, and the latter mostly through reservations. In all of these regimes, the application of secondary rules of international law, like the rules of treaty interpretation or rules of state responsibility, are generally not excluded by treaties. Hence, these secondary rules might result in the elevation of some legal protections enshrined in other sources of legal authority and result in contributory responsibility. Before discussing the operation of such arrangements in practice, below is a table summarizing this descriptive section:

---

that "the EU should pursue the creation of one permanent court" and offering some details regarding possible institutional features).

[185] See generally Colin M. Brown, *A Multilateral Mechanism for the Settlement of Investment Disputes. Some Preliminary Sketches*, 32 ICSID Rev.–For. Inv. L.J., REV.–FOR. INV. L.J. 673, 682 (2017) ("The EU is currently engaging on a similar basis with all of its negotiating partners (Viet Nam, Singapore, Japan, the United States, China, Myanmar, Indonesia, Malaysia, Mexico etc.)"). See also *Joint Interpretative Instrument on the Comprehensive Economic and Trade Agreement (CETA) between Canada and the European Union and Its Member States*, OJ L 11, 14 (Jan. 2017) (hereinafter CETA); European Commission Press Release, The EU and Vietnam Finalize Landmark Trade Deal (Dec. 2, 2015), at http://trade.ec.europa.eu/doclib/press/index.cfm?id=1409; European Commission Press Release, EU and Mexico Reach New Agreement on Trade (Apr. 21, 2018), at http://trade.ec.europa.eu/doclib/press/index.cfm?id=1830 ("the agreement . . . includes the EU's new Investment Court System").

TABLE 3.1[186] *Institutionalization of indigenous interests under economic regimes*

FIELD	INTEREST PROTECTED	LEGAL FORMS	EXAMPLES
Intellectual Property	– Cultural "Property" & Heritage – Collective Ownership	– Legal Obligations – Domestic Enforcement of Protections – Secondary Rules of IL	– Fair & Equitable Sharing of Benefits – Disclosure Requirements
Finance	– Self-Determination – Self-Governance	– Safeguards & Operational Policies – Secondary Rules of IL	– Impact Assessments Requirements – Free, Prior & Informed Consultation
Trade	– Social, Cultural & Religious Practices – Economic Preferences	– Exceptions, Reservations & Exemptions (Carve-Outs) – Secondary Rules of IL	– Preferential Treatment – Protection for Economic Development Initiatives
Investment	– Land & Natural Resources – Economic Preferences	– Reservations & Exemptions (Carve-Outs) – Secondary Rules of IL	– Exemption of Non-discrimination Requirements – Reserved Sectors

[186] Sergio Puig, *International Indigenous Economic Law*, 52 U.C. DAVIS. L. REV. 1243, 1290 (2019).

4

The Experience of Indigenous Peoples under Economic Regimes

How well do the provisions and safeguards of international economic arrangements achieve the goals of protecting the rights afforded to Indigenous peoples due to their conditions of subjugation and marginalization? The short answer is: not very well.

To unpack this answer in context, this chapter expands the survey of the treatment of Indigenous peoples in economic arrangements with examples illustrating the varied ways in which Indigenous peoples may interact with international economic law to protect or advance their interests. The examples are presented as "case studies." To some extent, the cases show how indigenous interests have used different arrangements to resist the cycle of susceptibility and exclusion created by economic interconnection or to take advantage of economic liberalization when possible. Some of the cases also incorporate my own experiences and perspectives working with different institutions between 2014 and 2019, thanks to Professor James Anaya, former United Nations Special Rapporteur on the Rights of Indigenous peoples, and a (former) colleague at the University of Arizona and during my visit at University of Colorado (where Professor Anaya sat as Dean of the Law School). Before this descriptive exercise, however, an important methodological caveat on the lessons that we can generalize from these cases.

4.1 A METHODOLOGICAL CAVEAT

The extent to which modern global frameworks of economic interconnection affect Indigenous peoples is an empirical question that is hard to answer, especially at a high level of specificity. In Chapter 2, I provided a general theory of a process (and some figures) that seeks to explain how the combined effects of such arrangements might be especially punitive or insensitive to the interests, values, rights and, most importantly, the general condition of indigenous groups throughout the world – exposing them to the negative effects of interconnected markets. If the diagnosis is a complex task, the assessment of the provisions designed to protect Indigenous peoples from such negative effects is a herculean one. Not only is it hard to attribute certain outcomes to a particular set of legal institutions when there is limited data, but it is often unclear what the specific goals of such provisions are and what criteria we should use to assess their effectiveness.

Moreover, whatever the goals of such legal institution might be, a key question for the assessment remains: compared to what? In other words, in critiquing or advocating a particular legal or institutional form or choice, one should not focus on the defects of a single institution or legal form while failing to apply the same rigor to its alternatives. Institutions (legal, markets or otherwise) should rather be assessed from a comparative perspective, one that avoids ideal characterizations in favor of analysis that takes account of real-life institutional pathologies. Just as Ronald Coase labeled economic analyses that compare an existing institution (say the legislative process) with an "ideal" alternative (say the market) as "blackboard economics," much international legal scholarship similarly fails to compare institutional alternatives, especially legal processes, that take account of their real-world complexity. In this context, this means that a very relevant question is the following: how much worse is the current process of globalization compared to other prior forms of global economic interconnection? And, is it possible to compare the effects of the (neo)liberal processes with similar process of economic functioning and exploitation – for instance, colonialism and its main exploitative mechanisms (slavery, formalized racial discrimination.)?

In any event and without dismissing these complex methodological questions, the case studies do not attempt to explain the condition of marginalization of Indigenous peoples throughout the world, but to generate testable hypotheses that can be applied in the future. This could help to provide improvements on research that seeks to understand the role of international economic law in indigenous governance. Therefore, the general truth or fallacy of the impact of globalization and the role of (or lack thereof) protections against exploitation is not at issue – although we may all have a hunch that more, *much more*, needs to be done. Instead, the cases merely attempt to complement the formal description of rules and legal institutions and, to a lesser extent, explain the role of international economic arrangements in indigenous affairs "in action."

But as this picture is completed in suboptimal ways, three main issues must be acknowledged about the case study methodology deployed. First is the limitation to determine, through counterfactual reasoning, how representative the cases are of the way Indigenous peoples engage with the international economic system. In other words, it is extremely difficult to know the number of stories of reliance upon institutionalized processes of international economic law compared with the number of cases where Indigenous peoples are affected as a direct consequence of international economic arrangements and activities. The second is that this work is based on only eight case studies, which makes the extrapolation and generalization of the conclusions to other situations very limited at most. Finally, it is often hard to determine what the relevant actors were originally seeking to accomplish with the use of institutionalized processes. With this in mind, what follows is a series of vignettes, mostly involving cases in the Americas (the continent where I have more context) to describe the role of international economic law in indigenous legal struggles.

4.2 INTELLECTUAL PROPERTY

4.2.1 *The Kuna People*

Based on and consistent with international treaties, Panamanian law recognizes and provides various protections for Indigenous peoples.[1] On that basis, Panama adopted IP provisions that "protect the collective intellectual property rights and traditional knowledge of Indigenous peoples in their creations . . . as well as the cultural elements of their history."[2] Thus, Panama's Law 20 of 2000 recognizes and protects the collective nature of these cultural expressions, instead of solely protecting the creation of an individual or company. Consistent with this law, in 2003 Panama and Taiwan entered into an agreement which *inter alia* protects the access to each Party's genetic resources and the traditional knowledge developed by Indigenous people and local communities.[3]

The Kuna People are a vibrant indigenous group that make up the second largest in Panama. One of the most well-known cultural expressions of the Kuna is the *mola*, a unique textile typically designed and worn by Kuna

---

[1]   Panama, Ley No. 2 de 1938 (Law No. 2 of Sept. 16, 1938), https://utp.ac.pa/documentos/2010/pdf/kuna_yala.PDF (creating indigenous jurisdictions).

[2]   Special System for the Collective Intellectual Property Rights of Indigenous Peoples, Código Fiscal No. 24,083, act 20, ch. I, art. 1 (Gaceta Oficial 2000) (creating "a special system to register, promote and market [indigenous IP] rights, in order to highlight the social and cultural values of indigenous cultures and guarantee social justice for them").

[3]   Free Trade Agreement between the Republic of China and the Republic of Panama, art. 16.07, https://investmentpolicy.unctad.org/international-investment-agreements/treaty-files/2660/download.

women.[4] It is created by carefully sewing textiles of various colors into a design that reflects elements of nature, such as the figure of an animal or a plant. The *molas* are important elements of culture and trade. They are commercialized in boutiques and souvenir shops and can be found in most, if not all, tourist areas of Panama.[5]

The *mola's* popularity has also led non-Kuna to copy and imitate the designs and use them for commercial purposes.[6] In the case of products imported into Panama with designs imitating or copying that of the *mola*, a procedure has been established where customs officials contact the Kuna representatives and inform them of the products.[7] The Kuna experts then assess whether the products are an imitation and/or if the company or individual has a license to use the designs. If either one of the conditions is not met, the Kuna traditional authorities initiate a criminal action against those who are illegally using their designs and may also block the imports.[8]

To date, all cases have been settled by the authorities, but licensing deals have resulted in handsome royalties for the Kuna.[9] Moreover, for any party interested in using the designs for commercial purposes, a system has been created to negotiate directly with the Kuna traditional authorities. The agreement is registered before the Directorate General of Copyright under the Ministry of Commerce and Industries. If no licensing agreement exists, a proceeding may be initiated against the unauthorized users and imports, which can result in hefty penalties.[10]

In some ways, the Kuna's is an uncommon but rosy textbook case: A well-endowed tribe empowered by law may profit from the commercialization of

---

[4] Diana Marks, *Appropriating the Mola: Forms of Borrowing by Textile Artists*, 3 J. TEXTILE DESIGN RES. & PRAC. 87, 88 (2016).

[5] Lynn Stephen, *Culture As a Resource: Four Cases of Self-Managed Indigenous Craft Production in Latin America*, 40 ECON. DEV. & CULTURAL CHANGE 101, 108, 111 (1991).

[6] Irma de Obaldia, *Western Intellectual Property and Indigenous Cultures: The Case of the Panamanian Indigenous Intellectual Property Law*, 23 B.U. INT'L L.J. 337, 359 (2005) (hereinafter *Panamanian IP*) ("In the 1980s, the popularity of the *molas* prompted a wave of imported imitations that flooded the market").

[7] Law No. 20 of 2000 adds a subparagraph to Article 439 of the Administrative Code (Código Fiscal), which prohibits the importation of any "article that imitates, completely or partly, the workmanship of the traditional dress of Indigenous peoples, as well as said peoples." See Special System for the Collective Intellectual Property Rights of Indigenous Peoples, Código Fiscal No. 24,083, act 20, ch. VI, art. 17 (Gaceta Oficial 2000).

[8] Panama New Criminal Code, Second Book, tit. VII, ch. IV (Pan.). Specifically Arts. 274 and 275 address crimes against the Collective Rights of Indigenous Peoples and their Traditional Knowledge, https://www.oas.org/juridico/mla/sp/pan/sp_pan-int-text-cp.pdf.

[9] Interview with Kuna representative (Mar. 2017) (on file with author).

[10] See Obaldia, *supra* note 6, at 366–77.

its resources. When implemented correctly in domestic law, indigenous IP protections recognized internationally give way to the collective enjoyment of royalties from, among other resources, its cultural expressions.

4.2.2 *The San People*

The second case study is relatively old, but a well-documented. It is known to many indigenous rights advocates and IP scholars, yet perhaps obscure to most international economic law scholars and lawyers.[11]

The San People, an indigenous group living in the Namib Desert and Kalahari region of South Africa, Botswana, Angola and Namibia, are estimated at about 100,000 people.[12] Despite relatively recent empowering victories, including a land recognition agreement formally signed with the South African government, the communities are poor, with limited prospects of access to education, to health or to participation in the modern forms of economy.[13] In part a consequence of their environment and in part because their traditions, the San People have used the *hoodia* plant (known locally as "Ilhoba I-L-H-O-B-A," "ghaap" or "bobbejaanghaap") as an appetite suppressant for many centuries, especially during long expeditions for their hunting and gathering.

Although the properties of hoodia had been known since at least the 1980s, a research consortium of South Africa isolated the active ingredient of the hoodia plant, a compound called P57, which it then patented in the late 1990s. The active ingredient of the hoodia can be used as a food ingredient for "weight management."[14] The estimated market size for this type of product was calculated in excess of US $3 billion per year – although some dispute the

---

[11] R. Ostergard, M. Tubin & P. Dikirr, *Between the Sacred and the Secular: Indigenous Intellectual Property, International Markets and the Modern African State*, 44 J. Mod. Afr. Studs., 309–333 (2006).

[12] See generally ROBERT HITCHCOCK & DIANA VINDING (eds.) INDIGENOUS PEOPLES' RIGHTS IN SOUTHERN AFRICA (Copenhagen: IWGIA 2004). See also *Survival International "The Bushmen,"* visit https://www.survivalinternational.org/tribes/bushmen.

[13] David Stephenson, *San Reach Landmark IPR Benefit-Sharing Accord For Diet Pill*, CULTURAL SURVIVAL QUARTERLY MAGAZINE (Sept. 2003), visit https://www.culturalsurvival.org/publications/cultural-survival-quarterly/san-reach-landmark-ipr-benefit-sharing-accord-diet-pill. A recent victory for the San People has been when the industry behind the herbal tea *rooibos* agreed to pay a percentage of the money that is made to the Indigenous peoples who used the plant before production was industrialized. See *South Africa's Rooibos Tea Industry to Pay Khoisan People*, BBC NEWS, Nov. 1, 2019, visit https://www.bbc.com/news/world-africa-50261517.

[14] *PCT Notable Inventions: Hoodia Appetite Suppressant*, WIPO, visit https://www.wipo.int/pct/en/inventions/hoodia/index.html.

properties as well as the figures. At the time of the patenting, South Africa did not have a set of laws and policies envisaged by the CBD in place (in force since September of 1993). In part as a result of mounting pressure after this case, the South African Biodiversity Act of 2003, as well as an addendum to the South African Patent Act in 2005, recognized protections to traditional and indigenous knowledge.[15]

More importantly, in a controversial deal the patent holder CSIR – a subnational research entity of the South African government – licensed the rights to a private company known as Phytopharm. Phytopharm then sublicensed the product for \$21 million to Pfizer – a global pharmaceutical company. In the process of the land negotiations with the South African government just referred to, the San found out about the patent deal.[16] In June 2001, an NGO alerted the San "that a worldwide patent had been secured, and that the commercial rights to the IP (including further research, drug development, marketing, etc.) had been licenced." This triggered a long process of negotiation between the CSIR as patent holder and the San as the wronged "traditional knowledge holders" that led to a benefit sharing agreement. According to WIPO the agreement required CSIR to pay to the San 8 percent of all licensing payments received and 6 percent of all future royalties.[17] The agreement also brings the opportunity for the development of more innovative IP and corresponding economic benefits.

Another important aspect – beyond the groundbreaking benefit sharing agreement – is that this case helped to develop capacity and more indigenous protections in South Africa.[18] In part as a result of interactions with international organizations and NGOs involved in heritage protection spearheaded by UNESCO, and WIPO on Traditional Knowledge and Folklore, the San developed the capacity to promote their IP rights. The San leaders became more effective in articulating their demands, as IP rights to their heritage in all tangible and intangible forms, leading to more protections

---

[15] See *Leveraging Economic Growth through Benefit Sharing*, WIPO, Sept. 16, 2015, visit https://www.wipo.int/ipadvantage/en/details.jsp?id=2594. According to WIPO, "Although significantly belated, the efforts of SASI, WIMSA and NGOs played a role in influencing the creation of significant protection of indigenous knowledge in South Africa through the Biodiversity Act of 2003 ... The Biodiversity Act is complemented with an addendum to the South African Patent Act in 2005, which requires a patent applicant to state on oath whether the patent contains the use of or reference to any indigenous or traditional knowledge".

[16] *Id.*

[17] *Id.*

[18] *Id.*

and benefits, including to San paintings which adorn caves across Southern Africa.[19]

4.3.1 *The Huave People*

Mexico has a robust and diverse array of Indigenous peoples. In the "isthmus" (*istmo*) region of Oaxaca, a region that has been identified as optimal for the development of wind power, the Mexican government and a concessionaire financed by the IDB sought to build the largest wind farm in Latin America.[20] The then US $1 billion–plus project in San Dionisio del Mar attracted the attention of many international human rights authorities including the Inter-American Commission of Human Rights, the UN Special Rapporteur on the Rights of Indigenous Peoples and, most notably, the independent complaint mechanism, or ICIM, of the regional development bank.

According to an internal investigation by the IDB, "[it] did not ensure that the conditions to carry out consultation and good faith negotiations with indigenous communities affected by the project were met."[21] Based on these findings, the ICIM recommended that the project be closed and that it not be carried out in the area and in the manner originally envisaged. It also recommended drawing up a compensation plan for the harm caused to the affected Huave (or Ikojts) community in violation of the IDB's Policy on Indigenous peoples (OP-765).

Despite this decision, the Mexican government relocated a slightly modified version of the same project twenty miles inland to an area adjacent to the city of Juchitán de Zaragoza. This time, the Mexican government decided to

---

[19] See Anton Ferreira, S. *African Rock Art Offers Picture of Harmony*, REUTERS, Jan. 20, 2007, visit https://www.reuters.com/article/us-safrica-rock/s-african-rock-art-offers-picture-of-harmony-idUSL1074803020061122.

[20] For a summary of recommendations, see generally S. JAMES ANAYA, OBSERVACIONES DEL PROFESOR S. JAMES ANAYA SOBRE LA CONSULTA EN EL CONTEXTO DEL PROYECTO ENERGÍA EÓLICA DEL SUR EN JUCHITÁN DE ZARAGOZA 1, Feb. 23, 2015, http://fundar.org.mx/wp-content/uploads/2015/03/Juchitan-observaciones-Anaya.pdf. For a discussion of the broader context, see S. James Anaya & Sergio Puig, *Mitigating State Sovereignty: The Duty to Consult with Indigenous Peoples*, 67 U. TORONTO L.J. 435, 439–46 (2017) (hereinafter *Mitigating State Sovereignty*).

[21] INTER-AMERICAN DEV. BANK, COMPLIANCE REVIEW REPORT MAREÑA RENOVABLES WIND PROJECT 5, (2012) http://idbdocs.iadb.org/wsdocs/getdocument.aspx?docnum=40671375.

implement a consultation with the Zapotec People (or Ben 'Zaa) for what the authorities called a "new" project in Juchitán, but now without financing from the IDB. The project's background: the presence of well-known foreign investors like Mitsubishi International Corporation, Vestas Wind Systems A/S and Macquarie Group Limited in the concessionaire; the partnership of these investors with a federal government workers' pension fund; and a history of unresolved land tenure controversies, all made the situation volatile.[22] Today, litigation looms before the Mexican Supreme Court and the fate of the project is uncertain. The litigation involves whether the process of consultation with Indigenous peoples satisfied the required standards (especially in the light of the relocation of a project predetermined without any input by the Zapotec).[23]

In short, this example shows the tensions that arise between fostering finance for development projects and safeguarding Indigenous peoples. It shows how the interests and incentives of the state are more likely to be aligned with those of MNCs than those of Indigenous peoples, and how officials within development banks may sometimes ignore compliance with their own safeguards. More positively, it also shows the potential that such instruments have to impact investment decisions, especially when safeguard protections are well institutionalized and effectively applied. Finally, it shows how the source of funding projects ultimately can impact the well-being of Indigenous peoples.

4.3.2 *The Maasai People*

This case involves the WB safeguards, the best-known standards applicable for development financing by international development banks. Before discussing the case, the following contextual information is relevant. In 2016, as a prelude to the 2016 Environmental and Social Framework (or 2016 ESF) the WB issued a report with a summary of all the investigations by the Bank's Inspection Panel. The report noted that nineteen Panel cases involved indigenous peoples' issues, which covered fifteen countries in four regions. It concluded that consultations and broad community support, social assessments and customary rights were the issues most represented in these investigations. According to that report's main summary conclusions:

---

[22] ANAYA, *supra* note 20.
[23] See Jorge Carrasco Araizaga, *La Corte Atrae Amparo Sobre Energía Eólica en Zona Indígena de Oaxaca*, PROCESO, Jan. 10, 2018, https://www.proceso.com.mx/518021/la-corte-atrae-amparo-sobre-energia-eolica-en-zona-indigena-de-oaxaca.

- The Indigenous peoples Policy is among the more complex of the Bank's safeguards due to the rigorous criteria, sensitivities attached, and the requisite specialized expertise necessary for its full implementation. The fact that a significant percentage of the world's poor are indigenous points to the necessity of giving this policy the importance and significance it deserves.

- Most of the lessons presented in this report relate to the project preparation stage of the project cycle, clearly pointing to the importance of this stage in projects involving Indigenous peoples. "Getting it right" from the very start is imperative. Improved screening to capture Indigenous peoples' presence in the project area and the impacts of the project on their interests is needed from the outset, and should include a thorough understanding of their land- and resource-based cultures and livelihoods.

- Greater expertise needs to be deployed to capture the specificities of Indigenous peoples, their livelihoods and cultural attachment to lands and resources. This points to the need for strengthened technical capacity and continued capacity development for relevant Bank staff.

- The World Bank has responded positively to many of the Panel investigations by adjusting its practices and increasing attention to indigenous issues on the part of borrowers. For example, in the Democratic Republic of Congo (DRC), the Panel case led to the recognition of Pygmies as Indigenous peoples by both the government and the World Bank, resulting in new commitments to mainstreaming Indigenous peoples as a crosscutting theme across activities in the country, as well as community-managed forest concessions granted to IPs. In the Kenya Natural Resource Management Project (NRMP) and as a result of the Panel's investigation, the Bank hosted a dialogue with the government and affected IPs on customary land and resource rights with the aim of addressing legacy issues related to land rights and ownership.[24]

The case that follows relates to Kenya's Electricity Expansion Project. The project did not apply the new 2016 ESF, in particular safeguard 7 on "Indigenous peoples/Sub-Saharan African Historically Underserved Traditional Local Communities." The 2016 ESF entered into force in October of 2018. However, after consultation with Charles di Leva, Chief Counsel of the Environmental and International Law Practice Group in the World Bank,

---

[24] WB Inspection Panel, Emerging Lessons Series No. 2, Indigenous Peoples, Oct. 2016, http://documents.worldbank.org/curated/en/447361478156710826/pdf/109710-REVISED-PUBLIC-IP-lessons-text-10-31-16web-links.pdf.

I determined that this case reflects best the lessons summarized in the report and is illustrative of the functioning, utility and role of safeguards and enforcement mechanisms. It is also a case in which I personally had a bit more context than any other recent case, as two of my advisees at the University of Arizona – Elifuraha (Eli) Laltaika and Paul Kanyinke Sena – studied and wrote about this case in their respective dissertations.

* * *

For centuries, the Maasai People who live in what today constitutes Tanzania and Kenya have had access to Lake Naivasha (in northern Kenya), a freshwater lake that fosters a rich environment, particularly important for the pastoralist Maasai who rely on the adjacent lands. The nearby Longonot Mountain has significant religious and ritual importance for the tribe too. In that area, the WB has supported geothermal generation since the early 1980s. A 2010 project, amounting to the equivalent of US $330 million in partnership with the European Investment Bank and other co-financiers, was developed for increasing the capacity, efficiency and quality of electricity supply, and to expand access to electricity in urban, peri-urban and rural areas of Kenya.

For the geothermal power generation component of the Project (one of four components) to be viable, a Maasai community (approximately 1,170 people) "agreed" to be resettled on the condition it would receive communal land title. did the community not obtain such a title, but the lands received were of inferior quality and less suitable for the pastoralist tribe. This and other complaints triggered an investigation that the Bank's Policies on Involuntary Resettlement, Indigenous peoples, Environmental Assessment and Natural Habitats were breached. Siding with the tribe, the WB's Inspection Panel concluded that in addition to lack of compliance with the Kenyan law regarding the benefit sharing of certain commercial investments, among other important good-practice approaches and related Bank policies that were not followed, the Bank failed in:

- Use the affected peoples' language, in this case the Maasai language, in the conduct of the census and other consultations with the community, including in written documentation, such as the PAP and census results.
- The inclusion of traditional structures of authority, specifically the group of Elders. Presentation of wider options to PAPs, for example with regard to housing construction types, materials and size, to fit different preferences better.
- The implementation of necessary livelihood restoration programs.

- The establishment of a comprehensive baseline of key socioeconomic indicators, and a monitoring system to assess progress in achieving resettlement goals throughout execution of the resettlement plan and to permit adjustments as needed.

This panel's finding led to a mediation process between the WB (and the other financiers), the Kenyan Government (through KenGen, the implementing agency) and the Maasai community. In noting the importance of such a process, the panel also stressed that, "Even with the best of intentions, as possessed by the stakeholders in the Project, and the best of planning (not necessarily evident throughout this Project and in any event always challenging), developments following resettlement must be closely monitored and corrective action taken as needed."[25] Through the WB's Grievance Redress Service (GRS) as co-facilitator, the meditation process led to an agreement, supported by "a clear majority" of the affected community as confirmed by observers from the Bank. It included corrective actions across different areas, including a process for determination of eligibility for resettlement compensation, capacity building for livelihood restoration, measures to repair and protect a water pipeline, improvement of roads, registration and issuance of the new land titles, fencing the cultural center and others.

A WB team closely monitored compliance with this and other commitments. This included several meetings and visits by the Bank's GRS. After nearly all actions in the program were concluded, "including transfer of the 1,500 acres of land to the Project affected people" the WB issued a last progress report on April 30, 2019. According to the WB, and as confirmed independently by a Maasai leader, the community expressed satisfaction with the way the GRS and the process took place and with the execution of the management action plan. Participants were particularly happy that the issue of land titles was resolved and with the compensations paid.

This example shows that even in this day and age, and after substantial experience developing and working with safeguards, the WB – a well-resourced IFI with many years of experience on this topic – still lacks capacity to apply safeguards to the specificities of indigenous peoples, their livelihoods and cultural attachment to lands and resources. It is unquestionable – at least to me, a former official of the WB – that there are incredibly competent, well-meaning professionals working to facilitate lending in compliance with safeguards at the WB. However, the level of mistakes evidenced in this project

---

[25] In response to the WB's Inspection Panel's findings and given that EIB had initiated a mediation process to help resolve the identified issues, Management proposed to the Board to participate in the EIB-sponsored mediation process, through the Bank's Grievance Redress Service as co-facilitator, instead of undertaking consultations on remedial actions in parallel.

suggests that the WB (as well as other IFIs) do not devote adequate resources to these issues and instead invest in other areas considered more relevant for the technical functioning of the Bank. It also shows that when determination exists (either as a result of attempts to correct mistakes or to avoid further embarrassment), those resources and leadership emerge – at least within the WB. It is under these conditions that the WB's Inspection Panel and GRS can have an especially meaningful role, as these enforcement mechanisms are there to provide some accountability and justice to the affected person. It is in the shadow of a functioning enforcement and justice system that safeguards tend to be more effective.

A final note on this case study is pertinent. The resolution of this case happened around the time that the African Court on Human and Peoples' Rights (African Court) delivered its decision on the Ogiek people case (May 2017). Like the Maasai, the Ogiek is a Kenyan community, and they were expelled from their ancestral lands in the Mau forest.[26] This much-celebrated decision was one of the first in the African Court to engage with the rights of marginalised communities; it showed an increasingly active legal community in the African human rights system and the potential of the African Charter (in particular, the right to nondiscrimination (Art. 2), culture (Art. 17(2) and (3)), religion (Art. 8), property (Art. 14), natural resources (Art. 21) and development (Art. 22)) to accommodate indigenous claims. Notably, the African Court read a duty to "effectively consult" into the right to development and the safeguard of "prior consultations" as a protective mechanism of the right to land.

4.4 TRADE

4.4.1 *The Inuit People*

The Inuit People of northern Canada, Greenland and Alaska have long considered seal hunting a part of their livelihood, culture and identity. In

---

[26] African Commission on Human and Peoples' Rights v. Kenya, No. 006/2012, Judgment, African Court on Human and Peoples' Rights [Afr. Ct. H.P.R.]. (May 26, 2017), http://www .african-court.org/en/index.php/55-finalised-cases-details/864-app-no-006-2012-african- commission-on-human-and-peoples-rights-v-republic-of-kenya-details. Other cases before the African human rights regional system have dealt with indigenous rights and dispossession by industrial activity involving foreign interests. Social and Economic Rights Action Center [SERAC] and Center for Economic and Social Rights [CESR] v. Nigeria, Communication 155/96, Afr. Comm'n H.P.R, ¶ 6 (May 27, 2002). The *Ogoni* case was concerned with a number of indigenous rights issues after the African Commission found that by permitting private oil companies (NNPC and SPDC) to damage the environment, Nigeria failed to protect the Ogoni people's rights.

2010, however, the European Union adopted a regulation banning the sale of both imported and European seal products.[27] In recognition of the degree to which seal hunting contributed to the subsistence of the Inuit, the EU ban included an exception specifically benefiting this group. This exception allowed the Inuit to sell their seal products within the EU so long as the products came from their traditional hunts. Interestingly, the exception only applied to the Inuit and not to other indigenous groups or to other hunters using similar methods.[28]

As a result, both the ban and the exception were challenged before a panel, and eventually the AB of the WTO, by countries with an interest in the EU's market. In particular, Canada and Norway argued that the ban discriminated against their industries, as it allowed seal products made by hunters in Greenland to more easily enter the EU's market, given the higher percentage of indigenous hunters in Greenland as compared to Canada or Norway.[29]

The EU defended its regulation as a necessary policy to protect public morals – a general justificatory exception permitted under WTO law.[30] While Canada conceded that the EU could issue a regulation to protect a widely held moral value, it argued that the EU could only do so after applying equivalent restrictions for indigenous and nonindigenous hunts. In its decision, the AB held that the EU ban failed to meet the requirement that the exception operate in a way that does not amount to arbitrary or unjustifiable discrimination. The AB was concerned about the measure's inconsistent approach, given that the EU did not seek to ameliorate the animal welfare conditions of indigenous hunts and that the exception meant that products from hunts that would otherwise be characterized as commercial could nevertheless slip in under the Inuit's exception. Lastly, the AB felt the EU could have done more to facilitate the access of Canadian Inuit to the exception.[31]

---

[27] European Parliament and Council Regulation (EC) 1007/2009, 2009 O.J. (L286) 36, available at http://trade.ec.europa.eu/doclib/docs/2009/november/tradoc_145264.pdf.

[28] *Id.* at 37–8.

[29] Request for Consultations by Canada, *European Communities – Measures Prohibiting the Importation and Marketing of Seal Products*, WT/DS400/1 (Nov. 2, 2009); Request for Consultations by Norway, *European Communities – Measures Prohibiting the Importation and Marketing of Seal Products*, WT/DS401/1 (Nov. 5, 2009). Request for Consultations by Canada, *European Communities – Certain Measures Prohibiting the Importation and Marketing of Seal Products*, WT/DS369/1 (Sept. 25, 2007).

[30] First Written Submission of the European Union, *European Communities – Measures Prohibiting the Importation and Marketing of Seal Products*, 199, 202, DS400, DS401 (Dec. 21, 2012), http://trade.ec.europa.eu/doclib/docs/2012/december/tradoc_150190.pdf.

[31] Appellate Body Report, *European Communities – Measures Prohibiting the Importation and Marketing of Seal Products*, paras. 5.320, 5.326, 5.337, 5.338, WTO Doc. WT/DS400/AB/R, WT/DS401/AB/R (June 18, 2014) (hereinafter *EC – Seal Products*).

Nevertheless, the decision left enough room so that "some modifications that would amount to gestures of good faith" could make the ban WTO-compliant.[32] In fact, today, Inuit produced seal products can enter the EU market after they are inspected by recognized bodies authorized by the Commission, enjoying privileged access to the common market.[33]

This case study shows how states can find themselves in legal jeopardy as a consequence of trade obligations when trying to regulate while protecting indigenous groups. While, in many cases, governments retain flexibility under the general exceptions, balancing elements – including proportionality and effectiveness – need to be asserted when governmental actions overly affect a particular class of products or producers. Still, the recognition by international trade authorities that regulating in favor of Indigenous peoples is a legitimate regulatory objective is an important step that provides additional tools to protect against challenges based on trade obligations.

4.4.2 *The Guarani-Kaiowá People*

The Guaraní-Kaiowá is a relatively small indigenous group, currently leaving the banishing forests of Paraguay, Brazil (mostly in the central west state of Mato Grosso do Sul) and Argentina (northeastern).[34] Kaiowá Guarani are being killed or disposed of their ancestral territory and of their material and cultural existence to enhance sugar, cattle and timber production – three significant export products of Brazil. Especially in Brazil, "[t]he rights of Indigenous peoples and environmental rights are under attack," according to UN Special Rapporteur on the rights of Indigenous peoples, Victoria Tauli Corpuz.[35] Experts have also noted that Brazil has seen the highest number of

---

[32] Rob Howse, Joanna Langille & Katie Sykes, *Sealing the Deal: The WTO's Appellate Body Report in EC – Seal Products*, AM. SOC'Y INT'L L. (2014), https://www.asil.org/insights/volume/18/issue/12/sealing-deal-wto%E2%80%99s-appellate-body-report-ec-%E2%80%93-seal-products.

[33] See *id*.

[34] The Guarani people in Brazil are divided into three groups: Kaiowá, Ñandeva and M'byá, of which the largest is the Kaiowá, which means "forest people," see Ana Valeria et al., *Indigenous Peoples in Brazil: The Guarani; A Case for the UN*, CULTURAL SURVIVAL QUARTERLY MAGAZINE, March 1994, visit https://www.culturalsurvival.org/publications/cultural-survival-quarterly/indigenous-peoples-brazil-guarani-case-un.

[35] See *A Death Foretold in Brazil – UN Expert Condemns Indigenous Peoples Killings and Urges an End to Violence*, UN-OHCHR, visit https://www.ohchr.org/EN/NewsEvents/Pages/DisplayNews.aspx?NewsID=20158&LangID=E.

killings of environmental and land defenders of any country over the last fifteen years, up to an average of about one every week![36]

Against this backdrop and amidst the negotiation of an international trade deal between the Mercosur (which include the three named countries plus Uruguay) and the European Union, the European Parliament issued a resolution on the situation of the Guarani Kaiowa people in November 2016. Such resolution "[s]trongly condemn[ed] the violence perpetrated against Indigenous peoples and communities in Brazil, and asks for an urgent solution of the humanitarian crisis that the Kaiowá Guarani people are facing."[37] Despite this resolution and UN warnings, instead of strengthening institutional and legal protection for Indigenous peoples, Brazil continued "weakening" many of the existing protections or ignoring their application."[38] In response and understanding the interest of Brazil in the trade deal with the single largest common market, the EU aggressively demanded, among others, the inclusion in such deal of protection and acceptance by Mercosur of provisions to foster sustainable development, and to shape global trade rules in line with shared values of democracy, human rights and the rule of law.[39]

While Brazil resisted specific provisions linking trade benefits to the enhancement of indigenous rights, the current (and possibly final) version of the Association Agreement will contain what is characterized by the EU as a solid framework to address human rights issues.[40] This framework includes provisions relating to the adoption of high standards to prevent the role of MNC in human rights violations.[41] However, in this framework, indigenous

---

[36] UN Sustainable Development Goals, *Indigenous and Environmental Rights under Attack in Brazil, UN Rights Experts Warn*, June 8, 2017. *UN Rights Expert Urges Brazil Not to Evict Guarani and Kaiowá Indigenous Peoples from Their Traditional Lands*, UN OHCHR (Aug. 11, 2015).

[37] European Parliament resolution of November 24, 2016 on the situation of the Guarani-Kaiowá in the Brazilian state of Mato Grosso do Sul, http://www.europarl.europa.eu/doceo/document/TA-8-2016-0445_EN.html. European Parliament resolution on the situation of the Guarani Kaiowa people in Brazil, http://www.europarl.europa.eu/doceo/document/B-8-2016-1260_EN.html?

[38] Jenny Gonzales, *Brazil Ignored UN Letters Warning of Land Defender Threats, Record Killings*, Mar. 23, 2018, visit https://news.mongabay.com/2018/03/brazil-ignored-u-n-letters-warning-of-land-defender-threats-record-killings.

[39] Interview with Brazilian negotiator (Mar. 2019).

[40] European Parliament Briefing on International Agreements in Progress, *The Trade Pillar of the EU-Mercosur Association Agreement*, https://www.europarl.europa.eu/RegData/etudes/BRIE/2019/640138/EPRS_BRI(2019)640138_EN.pdf.

[41] Text of the EU-Mercosur Trade Agreement: Trade and Sustainable Development, visit https://trade.ec.europa.eu/doclib/cfm/doclib_section.cfm?sec=151.

peoples' rights would be protected as part of general human rights only – and such protections within the trade agreement have been linked to other international instruments.[42] Despite this, a provision – Article 8 of the chapter on trade and sustainable development – is notable as it responds to some of the concerns over the business practices with respect to natural resources available in forests, which have caused violence against groups like the Kaiowá Guarani. The provision reads as follows:

Trade and Sustainable Management of Forests

1   The Parties recognise the importance of sustainable forest manage-
     ment and the role of trade in pursuing this objective and of forest
     restoration for conservation and sustainable use.
2   Pursuant to paragraph 1, each Party shall:

     . . .

(b)   promote, as appropriate and with their prior informed consent, the
      inclusion of forest-based local communities and Indigenous peoples in
      sustainable supply chains of timber and non-timber forest products, as
      a means of enhancing their livelihoods and of promoting the conser-
      vation and sustainable use of forests.[43]

It is unclear what changes in behaviour this provision will instigate. It is clear, though, that the provision included in the Association Agreement is far from the more sweeping carve-out adopted by the New Zealand government to protect the Maori. However, the case identifies specific benefits that can be allocated to address specific vulnerabilities by indigenous groups as well as how market access can be a powerful incentive. Even in the context of a powerful player like the Brazilian government, market access in trade deals can be used to leverage the relatively weak position of small groups like the Kaiowá Guarani. This indigenous group has suffered at the hands of violent ranchers or as a consequence of the systemic violence and economic policies and export interests of Brazil.

---

[42] See e.g., Trade and Responsible Management of Supply Chains, Pursuant to paragraph 1, each
      Party shall:
         (a) support the dissemination and use of relevant international instruments that it has
      endorsed or supported, such as the ILO Tripartite Declaration of Principles concerning
      Multinational Enterprises and Social Policy, the UN Global Compact, the UN Guiding
      Principles on Business and Human Rights and the OECD Guidelines for
      Multinational Enterprises.
[43] Text of the EU-Mercosur Trade Agreement *supra* note 40.

4.5 INVESTMENT

4.5.1 *Two North American Tribes*

At least two recent proceedings involving the United States have dealt with the intersection between foreign investor and indigenous rights.[44] The first case demonstrates typical impacts international investment regimes can have on Indigenous peoples. Briefly, the case involved the denial of a mining permit by the federal government due, in part, to the project's effect on the Quechan People's natural resources and cultural heritage. The denial was challenged by a Canadian investor as a measure "tantamount to expropriation of an investment."[45] In the end, the investor-state tribunal adjudicating the case found the governmental actions to be consistent with international law, but – as it is common among ISDS tribunals – did not substantively address the interesting points of view expressed by the Quechan Nation in its *amicus curiae* submission.[46]

A less typical case is *Grand River v. United States*, another NAFTA arbitration.[47] This proceeding dealt with a surviving claim from the tobacco Master Settlement Agreement – a settlement between authorities and companies in the United States resulting from deceptive practices in the promotion of tobacco products.[48] According to the claimants (Canadians, members of the Six Nations of the Iroquois Confederacy or "Haudenosaunee" People and investors in companies in the tobacco distribution sector), these measures affected their sales and constituted an expropriation of a substantial portion of the value of their investment. The tribunal had little sympathy for the claim, finding that the claimants had not been deprived of ownership or control of their business of distributing cigarettes in Native American territories (exempted from the Master Settlement Agreement).[49]

---

[44] The "suspended" case brought by TransCanada would have illustrated and tested a more troubling tension between the duty to consult and investment law. See TransCanada Corp. v. United States, ICSID Case No. ARB/16/21, Notice of Intent to Submit a Claim to Arbitration (Jan. 6, 2016), https://www.italaw.com/sites/default/files/case-documents/ITA%20LAW%207030 .pdf.

[45] See North American Free Trade Agreement, Can.-Mex.-U.S., art. 1102, Dec. 17, 1992, 32 I.L.M. 612, 641 (1993) ("Canada reserves the right to adopt or maintain any measure denying investors of another Party and their investments, or service providers of another Party, any rights or preferences provided to aboriginal peoples.") [hereinafter NAFTA Annex].

[46] See Glamis Gold, Ltd. v. United States of America, Award, at 3, 353 (June 8, 2009), https://www .italaw.com/sites/default/files/case-documents/ita0378.pdf.

[47] Grand River Enters. Six Nations, Ltd. v. United States of America, NAFTA/UNCITRAL Arb., Award (Jan. 12, 2011), https://www.italaw.com/sites/default/files/case-documents/ita0384.pdf.

[48] Sergio Puig, *Tobacco Litigation in International Courts*, 57 HARV. INT'L L. J. 383, 394–96 (2016).

[49] Grand River Enters. Six Nations, Ltd., Award, paras. 137–45.

Interestingly, the claimants in *Grand River* also contended that the customary international law standard of equitable treatment incorporates the duty to consult with Indigenous peoples. Accordingly, this barred the United States from removing special tobacco-related benefits "without first attempting to ameliorate the resulting impact upon Claimants as [indigenous] investors."[50] In the decision, the NAFTA tribunal recognized the existence of customary international law norms concerning Indigenous peoples, including "the right to be consulted with respect to any project that may affect them."[51] Nevertheless, it held that the norm does not require consultations with *individual investors*, but with Indigenous peoples through their traditional authorities.[52] This language indicates that the tribunal (with James Anaya as a member) was well aware of a relationship between the duty to consult and international investment law, as well as conscious of the proper scope of application of the duty to consult as a protection against *human rights* violations.[53]

These two cases show some of the potential interactions between the investment regime and indigenous rights. In particular, they show how investment law can empower MNCs to seek compensation when governments act against their interests and in favor of tribes. In some cases, especially when investors deal with less powerful governments, investment frameworks even over-empower multinational corporations by deterring actions that might give rise to investment claims by foreign investors.[54] At the same time, it could be said that such legal frameworks affect the capacity of governments to comply with their other obligations, including implementing human rights and engaging in innovative policymaking to address changing social, economic and environmental conditions that impact indigenous interests. Finally, the cases show how investment tribunals – when sensitive to indigenous rights – can help to contextualize the tension between investor and indigenous rights by reading investment treaties within a larger body of international law. And,

---

[50] See Susan L. Karamanian, *The Place of Human Rights in Investor-State Arbitration*, 17 LEWIS & CLARK L. REV. 423, 431 (2013).

[51] See Grand River Enters. Six Nations, Ltd., Award, para. 210 (quoting ILA Committee on the Rights of Indigenous Peoples, Interim Report (2010).

[52] See Karamanian, *supra* note 50 (citing Grand River Enters. Six Nations, Ltd., Award).

[53] See *id.* It is possible that business actors try to use investment treaties as a basis of state responsibility vis-à-vis the investor for consultations (or lack thereof) with Indigenous peoples. Such action could result in international responsibility on the part of the state only in very rare cases. *Mitigating State Sovereignty*, *supra* note 20, at 463.

[54] For examples of this imbalance and recommendations, see James Anaya (Special Rapporteur on the Rights of Indigenous Peoples), *Extractive Industries and Indigenous Peoples*, U.N. Doc. A/HRC/24/41 (July 1, 2013).

in some cases, indigenous foreign investors (or companies owned by indigenous investors) may also use the investment regime to protect their interests – although, admittedly, this is not a common or unchallenging use of the regime.

4.5.2 *The Sawhoyamaxa People*

There are multiple cases before ISDS tribunals involving indigenous groups. In some cases, indigenous groups seek participation as third parties to the dispute. In most instances, the argument expressed in those cases involves seemingly "competing" or "overlapping" state obligations toward different right-holders – foreign investors and indigenous groups. Examples of these are multiple and include Bear Creek's failure to secure the consent of indigenous communities, leading to the unrest of the community and ultimately Peru's "wrongful" termination of a concession.[55] In that case, Peru was ordered by the ISDS tribunal to compensate the investor.

The economic marginalisation of indigenous groups combined with the structure of international investment law (which grants no direct standing other than to claimant investor or respondent states) has consequences. Arbitrators are constrained by the matters raised by the parties and therefore unable directly to assign international responsibility for the violation of indigenous rights (except for limited circumstances). Moreover, like in the cases of *Bernhard von Pezold & Others v. Republic of Zimbabwe* and *Border Timbers Ltd. v. Republic of Zimbabwe,* investment tribunals are often prompt to reject third party participation of indigenous advocates (in these cases on behalf of the Chikukwa, Nogorima, Chinyai and Nyaruwa peoples from the Chimanimani region) for "apparent lack of independence or neutrality." Of course, there are notable exceptions, like the tribunals in *Glamis Gold v. United States* or the same Bear Creek case.

To be sure, there is another side of the coin to these cases. Before multiple regional human rights bodies – like the IACtHr, the African Commission of HR or the ACJ – a similar tension between the rights of corporations and the rights of Indigenous people is not infrequently observed. In other words, these bodies will often have to analyze whether a private, foreign investor was implicated in the alleged violation of human rights obligations toward

---

[55] In a nontraditional case, Chevron's request to be released of responsibility for the environmental impact, including toward "indigenous culture" as a result of the partnership or concession with Ecuador, Lise Johnson, *Case Note: How* Chevron v. Ecuador *Is Pushing the Boundaries of Arbitral Authority,* INV. TREATY NEWS (Apr. 13, 2012), https://www.iisd.org/itn/2012/04/13/case-note -how-chevron-v-ecuador-is-pushing-the-boundaries-of-arbitral-authority.

Indigenous peoples. These cases include the following: in *SERAC v. Nigeria*, the African Commission found that by permitting private oil companies to irreparably affect the Ogoni's land, Nigeria failed to protect the Ogoni people from Shell Oil Company. In the *Mayagna (Sumo) Awas Tingni Community v. Nicaragua*, the IACtHR decided that the granting of a thirty-year logging concession on indigenous land to the subsidiary of a South Korean company violated indigenous rights. And in the famous *Saramaka v. Suriname* the same regional court found that the granting of logging concessions to Chinese investors caused damage to the sustainable use of the forest that was inextricably linked to the survival of the Maroon. In all these cases, what was at stake was the responsibility of the state and not the investor; the international bodies have limited tools to sanction investors, even in these human rights mechanisms.

The following case – the *Sawhoyamaxa Indigenous Community v. Paraguay* – before the IACtHR involves precisely this later situation where a regional body assesses competing obligations. It has been analyzed by indigenous and investment law scholars alike. However, most analysis has missed some important nuances of the relationship of different bodies of law that are important especially in the light of the "innovative" argument rendered by the Colombian Constitutional Court in the judgment C-252/19.

* * *

The Sawhoyamaxa indigenous community was evicted from its traditional lands in the Paraguayan Chaco in the 1990s. The *Sawhoyamaxa v. Paraguay* case involved a claim by this group that Paraguay did not address, among other things, territorial rights claims over their ancestral land, then pending since 1991. This omission from addressing the claims and from restoring the possession of their property resulted in a state of nutritional, medical and health vulnerability, according to experts and the tribe. In a celebrated decision, the Court found that Paraguay was in breach of its obligations under numerous provisions of the Inter-American Convention on Human Rights, including Article 21, the human right to property.

In the dispute before the regional court, Paraguay argued unsuccessfully that the failure to restore the tribe's property was because the new owners have rights "protected under a bilateral agreement between Paraguay and Germany [,] which ... has become part of the law of [Paraguay]." Addressing this argument and interpreting investment obligations of the state in the light of human rights commitments, the Court decided succinctly as follows:

with regard to the third argument put forth by the State, the Court has not been furnished with the aforementioned treaty between Germany and Paraguay, but, according to the State, said convention allows for capital investments made by a contracting party to be condemned or nationalized for a "public purpose or interest", which could justify land restitution to Indigenous people. Moreover, the Court considers that the enforcement of bilateral [investment] treaties negates vindication of non-compliance with state obligations under the American Convention; on the contrary, their enforcement should always be compatible with the American Convention, which is a multilateral treaty on human rights that stands in a class of its own and that generates rights for individual human beings and does not depend entirely on reciprocity among States.[56]

Most commentators have noted that this decision stands for the proposition that Paraguay was required to comply with the obligations under both treaties: by making restitution in one instance (under the American Convention) and paying compensation in the other (under the Germany–Paraguay BIT). However, the case also stands for the proposition that BITs should be read in a compatible way with human rights obligations, which to the Court seem to have a higher status – a class of its own – among international obligations. This reading that implies the necessary compatibility of investment treaties with provisions of higher order, including Constitutional rights like equality has been recently espoused, developed and clarified by the Colombian Constitutional Court in the lucid judgment C-252/19. In its more relevant paragraph, it reads:

> the Court advises caution since a certain clause may allow for several interpretations, at least one of which may be incompatible with the Political Constitution. In this case, the appropriate remedy is to declare the conditional constitutionality [*exequibilidad condicionada*] of the treaty or any of its articles, then issue a warning to the President of the Republic such that if, in exercise of the constitutional competence to direct international relations, the President should decide to ratify the treaty, he must take the necessary steps to promote the adoption of a joint interpretative declaration with the representative of the other Contracting Party(s) regarding the conditions set by the Court in relation to the treaty or any of its articles. This, of

---

[56] *Sawhoyamaxa Indigenous Cmty., Merits, Reparations and Costs, Judgment, Inter-Am. Ct. H.R.* (ser. C.) No. 146, T 136. See also, Amnon Lehavi & Amir N. Licht, *BITs and Pieces of Property*, 36 Yale J. Int'l L. (2011).

course, lies within the framework of Article 31 of the Vienna Convention on the Law of Treaties.[57]

Unlike the IACtHR, the Colombian Court acknowledged that the broad provisions of BITs can lead to problematic interpretations in direct conflict with human rights obligations – hence the conditionality in their validity. In particular the court identified terms in the text of the BIT relating to fair and equitable obligations – "in conformity with international law," "*inter alia*" and "legitimate expectations" – as potentially problematic. This is a recognition of the complexities of granting expansive rights to investors, interpreted by *ad hoc* tribunals frequently with little or no understanding of indigenous rights. To some extent it is also a hint that such expansiveness and application can often come at the cost of the rights of other stakeholders, including local communities. Therefore, a lesson from the Sawhoyamaxa case in the light of this recent decision is the need for dialogue regarding the impact of BITs on indigenous national and human rights systems. While the compatibility must be presumed, interpretations that deviate are textually (and contextually) possible. These should be avoided for the protection of Indigenous peoples, who are especially vulnerable to the structural aspects of international investment law as these cases demonstrate.

---

[57] Colombian Constitutional Court Judgment C-252/19 (July 2, 2019), https://www.corteconstitucional.gov.co/relatoria/2019/c-252-19.htm#_ftn233 (para. 68).

5

The Recalibration of Indigenous Rights
and Economic Law

In Chapter 2 of this book, I provided a theory of the impact of the modern institutions of globalization on Indigenous peoples – what I called the process of susceptibility and exclusion. In Chapter 3, instead, I described the way these business and economic law frameworks have slowly adapted to address the rights and interests of Indigenous peoples. Chapter 4 complemented such a picture with eight case studies that implicate international economic regimes and looked more closely at the application and operation of such protective provisions.

In this chapter, I assess the intersection – that between international economic law and indigenous rights – which I have called international indigenous economic law. I argue that there is an important place for indigenous rights within the field of international economic law. As I explain, an international indigenous economic law, one that focuses on the vulnerable and marginalized, can provide a limited yet important pathway for improving the unequal distribution of the benefits of globalization and for moving beyond the standard conversations among mainstream and classical economists and policymakers that the redistribution of wealth and power should be purely domestic policy responses. This claim has implications for international economic law and indigenous rights scholars alike.

The chapter is divided into two sections to dissect such implications. In the first section, I note that when indigenous law scholars have studied the harms of globalization on Indigenous peoples, they tend to turn to human rights law to solve them, and, in this process, they also often treat international economic law (and its institutions) as a threat. Based on what I call normative and jurisprudential impacts, I argue that while shortcomings in the handling of Indigenous people's rights and interests by these frameworks remain, this skepticism ignores valuable tools, including those that might be more helpful in enforcing obligations upon non-state actors than traditional human rights instruments. Concretely, these mechanisms enable or help (1) to expose the negative effects of the operations of MNCs on indigenous communities; (2) to strengthen the capacity of states and international organizations to protect indigenous rights; (3) to condition economic benefits on the support of indigenous interests; and (4) to provide policy incentives that promote indigenous products and the practices associated with their production.

In contrast, in the second section of this chapter, I suggest that international economic law scholars have too largely ignored indigenous rights, or at best treat them as interesting exceptions to international economic law without much purchase. This is problematic not only because it has made us less sensitive to the struggles of vulnerable populations but this framework has limited our understanding of the ways in which international economic law is implicated in the process of susceptibility and exclusion of indigenous and nonindigenous communities around the world. More importantly it also has resulted in a blind spot when drawing lessons of how indigenous rights are transforming the field – for the better. In particular, this lack of systematic engagement with the international indigenous economic law obscures three potentially transformational impacts that should serve as a (broad) guide for the improvement of international economic law at an important, possibly disruptive time of globalization. These three impacts are: (1) the incorporation of new standards, metrics and tools available in international economic treaties; (2) the modification of the practice of international economic lawmaking; (3) the use of international economic arrangements to lock in social and economic policy for vulnerable and/or marginalized populations.

5.1 NORMATIVE AND JURISPRUDENTIAL IMPACTS

International law is intersectional; though its specialized fields operate independently, they intersect and connect.[1] To address the most negative effects of globalization, an effort that becomes increasingly urgent as the frustration among many communities becomes gradually more obvious, a better

---

[1] See, e.g., Ahmadou Sadio Diallo (Guinea v. Dem. Rep. Congo), Compensation, Judgment, I.C.J. Reports 2012, 324, 391, para. 8 (separate opinion by Greenwood, J.) ("International law is not a series of fragmented specialist and self-contained bodies of law . . . it is a single, unified system of law"); Johanna E. Bond, *International Intersectionality: A Theoretical and Pragmatic Exploration of Women's International Human Rights Violations*, 52 EMORY L.J. 71 (2003); Joost Pauwelyn, *Human Rights in WTO Dispute Settlement*, in HUMAN RIGHTS AND INTERNATIONAL TRADE 205 (Thomas Cottier et al. eds., 2005) (hereinafter *Human Rights*) (examining ways in which the WTO accounts for human rights in trade dispute settlement).

understanding of these intersections and connections is required. Specifically, it is essential to understand the intersection between international economic law – a field that emphasizes the expansion of transnational finance, trade and investment volumes and fosters economic activity, development and growth – and "human-focused" bodies of public international law, particularly human rights law – a field that emphasizes equality before the law, the prevention of social conflicts and the development of human capabilities.

As illustrated already and explained in more detail shortly, this body of law has a distinct normativity, which serves not only to reinforce the liberties and protections granted to economic actors, but also: (1) to expose the negative effects of the operations of MNCs on indigenous communities; (2) strengthen the capacity of states and international organizations to protect indigenous rights; (3) condition economic benefits on the support of indigenous interests; and (4) provide policy incentives that promote indigenous products and the practices associated with their production.[2] To more fully explain these functions, I consider this intersection – international indigenous economic law – applied first as a shield for the protection of indigenous rights and then as a sword for their advancement.[3]

5.1.1 *A Shield for Indigenous Rights*

Both customary international law and painstakingly negotiated instruments impose on state and non-state actors (including IFIs) a comprehensive set of duties designed to protect Indigenous peoples.[4] When these instruments are invoked before international economic institutions, they operate as a defensive shield for the protection of indigenous rights. But the four main regimes of international economic law incorporate these protections in varying ways,

---

[2] For a description of the potential uses of trade law, see, e.g., Philippe Sands, *"Unilateralism,"* Values and International Law, 11 EUR. J. INT'L L. 291 (2000). For investment law, see, e.g., Charles H. Brower II, *Corporations As Plaintiffs Under International Law: Three Narratives about Investment Treaties*, 9 SANTA CLARA J. INT'L L. 179, 209–10 (2011). For finance law, see, e.g., PROTECTING THE INDIVIDUAL FROM INTERNATIONAL AUTHORITY (Monika Heupel & Michael Zürn eds., 2017).

[3] For a discussion of health and human rights as a shield and sword, see Harold Hongju Koh, *Global Tobacco Control as a Health and Human Rights Imperative*, 57 HARV. INT'L L.J. 433, 433–47 (2016).

[4] See generally W. Michael Reisman, *Protecting Indigenous Rights in International Adjudication*, 89 AM. J. INT'L L. 350 (1995); Siegfried Wiessner, *Rights and Status of Indigenous Peoples: A Global Comparative and International Legal Analysis*, 12 HARV. HUM. RTS. J. 57 (1999).

and, in each regime, the goal of advancing indigenous rights meets varying levels of success.

The particular mechanism of indigenous protection under a given economic regime – trade, investment, IP or finance – reflects not only its distinct historical context, but also its particular nature and operational structure. For instance, the IP regime, concerned primarily with the unfair exploitation of indigenous cultural and biological resources, establishes special procedures to insulate these resources from the market forces and commoditization that the regime might otherwise unleash and in some cases, recognizes a right to enjoy benefits. While the regime provides limited enforcement at the international level, it encourages domestic processes and causes of action for the protection of indigenous resources and to improve the collective bargaining position of Indigenous peoples.[5] The case of the Kuna People provides a clear example of the operation of the IP regime as a shield for the protection of indigenous rights. When a relatively well-endowed tribe is empowered by law it can also profit from the commercialization of its resources. Hence, international economic law must find ways to institutionalize indigenous IP protections that result in the collective enjoyment of royalties from indigenous expressions and other resources. As I explain shortly, the *San* case study goes shows the use of IP law as a sword in the sense that it allows for the recognition of a right to enjoy benefits from IP resources.

International finance, on the other hand, concerns itself with actualizing indigenous self-determination; building broad community support prior to the design and implementation of development projects; and enabling the monitoring and accountability of organization recipients of financing with standards or "safeguards" crafted with indigenous representatives. These safeguards, of course, operate with varying levels of success. At best, and as in the case of the Huave and the Maasai People, financial institutions can ensure that their funded projects uphold the protections these safeguards support. At worst, governments, international organizations and MNCs might ignore these safeguards with little threat of legal consequence. In fact, the *Maasai* case study, while positive in its final outcome, also shows a lamentable aspect of this intersection: even in this day and age, the WB – a well-resourced IFI with many years of experience on this topic – still lacks capacity to apply safeguards to the specificities of Indigenous peoples, their livelihoods and cultural attachment to lands and resources. Moreover,

---

[5]   See, e.g., General Assembly of the States Parties, *Operational Directives for the Implementation of the Convention for the Safeguarding of the Intangible Cultural Heritage*, UNESCO, June 6, 2014, visit https://ich.unesco.org/doc/src/ICH-Operational_Directives-5.GA-EN.docx.

institutions are often unable to constrain borrowers from obtaining financing that is not burdened with these safeguards – leaving their application to other legal regimes or voluntary CSR systems.

Finally, the fields of trade and investment rely primarily on exceptions. Such exception allow a state to defend actions that are reasonable efforts to protect indigenous rights or interests. In trade, these exceptions allow states to defend programs that favor indigenous products and the practices associated with their production. The case of the Inuit People exemplifies the use of such an exception, and shows that the flexibility to protect and grant advantages to Indigenous peoples, while not unlimited, does exist, and is increasingly recognized by governments and adjudicators in this legal domain. In international investment – a field with relatively few explicit protections – treaty reservations, exceptions and carve-outs focus on the protection of indigenous lands and natural resources. These protections insulate investment programs designed, or areas preserved for, indigenous autochthonous development. In certain limited instances, like the case brought by the Six Nations in *Grand River*, the rights of Indigenous peoples as economic participants in globalization might be enforced – an infrequent use of investment treaties that can complement other remedies and sources of legal authority. However, international investment law is characterized by granting expansive rights to investors, interpreted by *ad hoc* tribunals frequently with little or no understanding of indigenous rights. Therefore, a lesson from the *Sawhoyamaxa* case, in light of the recent decision by a Colombian Court, suggests the need for a dialogue regarding the impact of BITs on indigenous national and human rights systems.

These mechanisms prove that, in theory, when looked at through its relational capacity, international economic law already enjoys a minimum protective basis. This is achieved mostly through the operation of unilateral reservations, rule exceptions or policy carve-outs (exemptions) and the consequent application of international legal obligations through *secondary* rules of international law (those concerning and controlling how primary rules ought to be interpreted and applied), to protect Indigenous peoples against rights violations resulting from economic policy; or, in other words, to act as a shield for indigenous rights. Indeed, wielding the shield is difficult and costly for most indigenous groups. Essentially, it requires well-organized and well-informed communities, operating in a transaction-costly environment, to activate economic arrangements to prevent, protect, or (at a minimum) mitigate some of the most negative effects of globalization.

Nevertheless, there is a glimmer of hope that international economic law will be a more effective shield for indigenous rights in the future. For one, states have recognized an undeniable right under international law to protect the public interest through reasonable government action.[6] In the particular case of Indigenous peoples, governments as well as international organizations *must* do so, as different sources of international law demand effective actions in favor of this specially protected category of people. Though measures to protect the rights of Indigenous peoples *domestically* will no doubt be challenged, the unique recognition of Indigenous peoples by international law as politically vulnerable and economically marginalized justifies broad efforts to protect Indigenous peoples – in effect, significantly enlarging states' policy and regulatory space, as well as police powers.[7] Moreover, bodies like WIPO, WTO Panels, the AB and ICSID tribunals have offered a more expansive interpretive approach to relevant flexibilities included in treaty texts.[8] Notably, in past WTO cases, the AB had hinted that when "examining WTO claims, other human-focused bodies of public international law can offer a justification that precludes a panel from finding that WTO law has been breached."[9] In fact, in *EC-Seals*, the WTO drew an actual connection with the concerns of Indigenous peoples, effectively reading those concerns as a potentially suitable justification.[10] Similarly, in the investment terrain, recent decisions

---

[6] See, e.g., Henok Asmelash & Edoardo Stoppioni, *Balancing between Trade and Public Health Concerns: The Latest Step in the Plain Packaging Saga*, BLOG EUR. J. INT'L L. (2018), https://www.ejiltalk.org/balancing-between-trade-and-public-health-concerns-the-latest-step-in-the-plain-packaging-saga. See generally Joel P. Trachtman, *Institutional Linkage: Transcending "Trade and . . ."* 96 AM. J. INT'L L. 77, 77–8 (2002).

[7] See generally Markus Wagner, *Regulatory Space in International Trade Law and International Investment Law*, 36 U. PA. J. INT'L L. 1, 68 (2014) (concluding "that, under particular circumstances a state or a WTO member has discretion – within limits – to deny the (full) enjoyment of an investment or the importation of a particular product, provided that a justification can be provided").

[8] For WIPO, see, e.g., World Intell. Prop. Org., *Patent Related Flexibilities in the Multilateral Legal Framework and Their Legislative Implementation at the National and Regional Levels*, WIPO Doc. CDIP/5/4 (Mar. 1, 2010), http://www.wipo.int/meetings/en/doc_details.jsp?doc_id=131629. For WTO-Panels see, e.g., Panel Report, *European Communities – Measures Prohibiting the Importation and Marketing of Seal Products*, WTO Doc. WT/DS400/R, WT/DS401/R (Nov. 25, 2013). For ICSID tribunals see, e.g., Philip Morris Brands, Sàrl v. Oriental Republic of Uru., ICSID Case No. ARB/10/7, Award, paras. 235–307 (July 8, 2016), https://www.italaw.com/sites/default/files/case-documents/italaw7417.pdf.

[9] Koh, *supra* note 3, at 440 (citing Appellate Body Report, *United States – Import Prohibitions of Certain Shrimp and Shrimp Products*, para. 185, WTO Doc. WT/DS58/AB/R (Nov. 6, 1998).

[10] Panel Report, *supra* note 8, para. 7.296 ("[T]he interests to be balanced against the objective of the measure at issue are grounded in the importance, recognized broadly in national and international instruments, of the need to preserve Inuit culture and tradition and to sustain their livelihood").

by *ad hoc* tribunals have noted the importance of the intersection of international investment law with other fields of international law and have recognized the duty of governments to protect against human rights violations.[11] This recognition expands the capacity to utilize international economic law as a shield for the protection of indigenous rights.

The intersection of international economic law and indigenous rights or international indigenous economic law embraces a distinct normativity – one that above all, emphasizes the *defensive* nature of international law. The intersection recognizes that the materialization of the rights of Indigenous peoples is a legitimate reason to regulate business activities, to deny or suspend financial backing or to modify the standard operation of the protections offered to IP owners. That is, international indigenous economic law can and should operate as a shield for the protection of indigenous rights.

5.1.2 *A Sword for Indigenous Rights*

International indigenous economic law may also serve as a "sword" for the advancement of indigenous rights. This use of the intersection is only just emerging as part of a "jurisgenerative" moment in indigenous rights advocacy.[12] Its effectiveness, however, depends on active, organized and sustained use by states, international organizations and civil society groups and the ability of these actors to "foster bridges," including with international business lawyers.[13]

Indigenous peoples have traditionally relied on human rights regimes to challenge the laws, policies and practices of the states in which they reside.[14] Underutilized, however, are the *primary* rules of international law (those concerning and controlling a particular subject matter) of economic treaties, which can be relied on to effect those laws and policies *extraterritorially*.[15] For instance, clauses in economic agreements may justify the suspension of trade

---

[11] See Urbaser S.A. v. The Argentine Republic, ICSID Case No. ARB/07/26, Award, para. 1200 (Dec. 8, 2016), https://www.italaw.com/sites/default/files/case-documents/italaw8136_1.pdf (noting that the BIT being applied in that case "has to be construed in harmony with other rules of international law of which it forms part, including those relating to human rights").

[12] Kristen A. Carpenter & Angela R. Riley, *Indigenous Peoples and the Jurisgenerative Moment in Human Rights*, 102 CAL. L. REV. 173, 205–233 (2014).

[13] For a discussion about the prospects of human rights advocacy, see generally César Rodríguez-Garavito, *Reimagining Human Rights*, 13 J. INT'L L. & INT'L REL. 10 (2017).

[14] See S. James Anaya, *Indian Givers: What Indigenous Peoples Have Contributed to International Human Rights Law*, 22 WASH. U. J.L. & POL'Y 107, 108–109 (2006).

[15] See generally H. L. A. HART, THE CONCEPT OF THE LAW ch. 5 (1961) (distinguishing between primary and secondary rules).

benefits when business actors under the jurisdiction of treaty partners fail to comply with basic human rights.[16] This possibility has been clarified with recent treaty practice and jurisprudential developments at the WTO.[17]

Consider, for instance, a logging concession granted without satisfying the duty to consult with Indigenous peoples and that ultimately results in the gross violation of indigenous rights. If the trade agreement contains a human rights exception clause (not uncommon in EU treaty practice), a government could block imports of timber until the exporting state rights the violation.[18] At the WTO, where no such textual basis exists, the barriers may be justified as long as they meet the well-established conditions of the *chapeau*, which I explain shortly.

Deploying treaties to effect extraterritorial behavior is a step beyond utilizing them to protect residents from, say, tobacco harm, with antismoking legislation based on the Framework Convention on Tobacco Control.[19] In effect, this use allows a state to block market access or condition economic benefits on the adoption of certain behavior abroad, essentially forcing values on a community that may not hold them. The WTO-AB has laid the groundwork for a state to defend just this sort of extraterritorial imposition on "public morals" grounds.[20] A government might also be concerned in the compliance with human rights obligations that protect the lives, health and well-being of Indigenous peoples abroad. This, I would argue, grants a legitimate interest in the imposition of restrictions against goods, services or even investments and a reasonable affirmative defense under other general exemptions to justify the extraterritorial effects of a measure.[21] The USMCA protocol, while not concerned with indigenous rights, provides an accelerated arbitral mechanism to address alleged violations of labor obligations under the USMCA. Notably, sanctions such as increased tariffs are available on a fast track for individual enterprises found to have committed violations and that failed to correct them.

---

[16] See Pauwelyn, *Human Rights*, *supra* note 1, at 206.

[17] See, e.g., *EC — Seal Products*, *supra* note. *See* Appellate Body Report, *European Communities — Measures Prohibiting the Importation and Marketing of Seal Products*, paras. 5.320, 5.326, 5.337, 5.338, WTO Doc. WT/DS400/AB/R, WT/DS401/AB/R (June 18, 2014) [hereinafter *EC — Seal Products*].

[18] See LORAND BARTELS, HUMAN RIGHTS CONDITIONALITY IN THE EU's INTERNATIONAL AGREEMENTS ch. 6 (2005).

[19] WHO Framework Convention on Tobacco Control, May 21, 2003, 2302 U.N.T.S. 166.

[20] See e.g., *EC – Seal Products*, *supra* note 17, ¶ 2.28.

[21] In some instances, the state may even have a duty to act. For discussion, see U.N. Econ. & Soc. Council, Rep. of the U.N. High Commissioner for Human Rights, ¶ 12, U.N. Doc. E/2007/82 (June 25, 2007).

To be sure, without express text to the contrary, a unilateral, extraterritorial application must also satisfy at least two additional elements reflected in the introductory paragraph of Article XX of the GATT.[22] First, a state acting to enforce indigenous rights extraterritorially with trade measures must do so under the aegis of a widely subscribed international agreement or under customary international law.[23] Only such sources of legal authority provide a sufficient basis to justify the act. By all means states cannot act unilaterally to protect all values, only those that are basic to the operation and goals of the trading system. The Preamble of the Agreement establishing the WTO makes reference to two relevant purposes: the fulfillment of sustainable development, and the improvement of living standards, including (or especially, depending on one's view) for marginalized and/or vulnerable populations.[24] This reference allows for the consideration of multiple policy goals in the process of interpretation as part of the object-and-purpose analysis of the treaty text.[25]

---

[22] General Agreement on Tariffs and Trade art. XX, Oct. 30, 1947, 61 Stat. A-11, 55 U.N.T.S. 194 ("Subject to the requirement that such measures are not applied in a manner which would constitute a means of arbitrary or unjustifiable discrimination between countries where the same conditions prevail, or a disguised restriction on international trade").

[23] See Sands, *supra* note 2, at 299 (discussing this premise in the context of environmental law).

[24] See Marrakesh Agreement Establishing the World Trade Organization, Apr. 15, 1994, 1867 U.N.T.S. 154 ("Recognizing that . . . trade and economic endeavours should be conducted with a view to raising standards of living . . . and expanding the production of and trade in goods and services, while allowing for the optimal use of the world's resources in accordance with the objective of sustainable development"); Appellate Body Report, United States – Import Prohibition of Certain Shrimp and Shrimp Products, ¶ 12, WTO Doc. WT/DS58/AB/R (Oct. 12, 1998) (hereinafter U.S. Shrimp Report) (noting, in construing Article XX that a "purpose [that] is fundamental to the application of Article XX cannot be ignored [in light of the wording of] the preamble to the Marrakesh Agreement"); Makau Mutua & Robert Howse, *Protecting Human Rights in a Global Economy: Challenges for the World Trade Organization*, in HUMAN RIGHTS IN DEVELOPMENT YEARBOOK 1999/2000: THE MILLENNIUM EDITION 51, 62 (Hugo Stokke & Anne Tostensen eds., 2001) ("[T]he actual text of the GATT reflects the recognition of supervening non-trade public values which were meant to prevail in the event of conflict with the free trade rules in the GATT").

[25] U.S. Shrimp Report, *Id.*, ¶ 12 ("An environmental purpose is fundamental to the application of Article XX, and such a purpose cannot be ignored, especially since the preamble to the [WTO Agreement] . . . acknowledges that the rules of trade should be in accordance with the objective of sustainable development, and should seek to protect and preserve the environment"); see also Panel Report, *Brazil – Certain Measures concerning Taxation and Charges*, ¶ 7.568, WTO Docs. WT/DS472/R & WT/DS497/R (Aug. 30, 2017) (hereinafter *Brazil Taxation Panel Report*) ("The Panel therefore finds that Brazil has demonstrated that a concern exists in Brazilian society with respect to the need to bridge the digital divide and promote social inclusion, and that such concern is within the scope of 'public morals' as defined and applied by Brazil").

Moreover, competing values should be balanced in favor of the enjoyment of human rights (a *pro homine* principle).[26]

Second, a state attempting to act extraterritorially to protect indigenous rights should do so only after first pursuing diplomatic means for the accurate application of relevant rules or standards (for example, standards to implement the duty to consult under ILO 169).[27] Adjudicatory bodies – most notably, the WTO-AB in the *Shrimp-Turtle* dispute – have granted states leeway to choose a particular diplomatic action, as long as it fosters multilateral cooperation and is fairly applied.[28]

Additional possible offensive uses of international economic law and its institutions for the advancement of indigenous rights exist. Now consider a logging concession granted to a foreign investor complicit in the forcible removal of Indigenous peoples from their ancestral lands. If the project is funded by an IFI, "a foreign representative acting as the agent" of adversely affected Indigenous peoples like an NGO may force an independent investigation before the compliance system of that body.[29] If the financing body's panel confirms the violation of indigenous rights, it will commence remedial actions or even halt disbursements. Moreover, the foreign investor may be reasonably sanctioned and lose funding sources in its home state, as well as precluded from bringing a successful claim before an *ad hoc* tribunal (perhaps on admissibility grounds) if the operating permit, license or concession is canceled by the host state.[30] The host state may also bring a claim or counter-claim before an *ad hoc* tribunal for the alleged violation of human rights, if specific language exists in the contract or BIT – an emerging trend in

---

[26] See Robert Kolb, Interprétation et Creation du Droit International 54 (Brussels, Bruylant, 2006); Yota Negishi, *The Pro Homine Principle's Role in Regulating the Relationship between Conventionality Control and Constitutionality Control*, 28 Eur. J. Int'l L. 457, 459 (2017).

[27] See International Labor Organization (Convention No. 169) on Indigenous and Tribal Peoples [ILO Convention 169], art. 6.

[28] Panel Report, *United States – Import Prohibition of Certain Shrimp and Shrimp Products, Recourse to Article 21.5 by Malaysia*, ¶ 7.1, WTO Doc. WT/DS58/RW (June 15, 2001).

[29] The Inspection Panel for the International Bank for Reconstruction and Development, International Development Association: Operating Procedures, Aug. 19, 1994, 34 I.L.M. 510, 511 (as amended).

[30] Spentex Netherlands, B.V. v. Republic of Uzbekistan, ICSID Case No. ARB/13/26, (Dec. 27, 2016) (ruling that one purpose of the investment system is to promote the rule of law, which precluded offering protection to investors that engaged in unlawful activities) (not public). For information, see, Vladislav Djanic, *In Newly Unearthed Uzbekistan Ruling, Exorbitant Fees Promised to Consultants on Eve of Tender Process Are Viewed by Tribunal As Evidence of Corruption, Leading to Dismissal of All Claims under Dutch BIT*, IA Reporter (July 22, 2017), http://tinyurl.com/ybt2p8pr.

investment instruments.[31] In these ways, international economic institutions may sanction foreign investors who fail to comply with legal requirements enshrined in human rights norms.[32]

Finally, international economic law can be used to develop the social, economic or cultural activities of Indigenous peoples. Consider, for instance, provisions in IP regimes that allow states to condition the recognition of rights on the satisfaction of requirements that forward the cultural protection and economic development of Indigenous peoples. With some caveats, this possibility is also available in trade and investment regimes. The cases of the *San* and the *Guarani-Kaiowá People* demonstrates how specific benefits can be allocated to address specific vulnerabilities as well as how market access or IP protections can be a powerful incentive to share the economic benefits of global markets. And while international finance safeguards are protective in nature, their presence has triggered the inclusion of indigenous interests in financing and development programs by IFIs – opening economic opportunities, one may hope, for indigenous groups.[33]

In short, the emerging opportunities exist to use international indigenous economic law as a sword. Despite often being criticized by indigenous advocates, the instruments and institutions of international economic law offer a complementary normativity – one that enables the "offensive" use of international law to strengthen indigenous communities.[34] Indigenous advocates in coordination with states, international organizations, MNCs and international economic law practitioners should utilize these tools, even if they come from outside the contours of what is traditionally defined as human

---

[31] See e.g., CPTPP, art. 9.19.2; NEW ZEALAND FOREIGN AFF. & TRADE, INVESTMENT AND ISDS FACT SHEET 4, http://www.tpp.mfat.govt.nz/assets/docs/TPP_factsheet_Investment.pdf ("The Government is expressly permitted to make a counterclaim and obtain damages when the investor is in the wrong under a covered investment agreement").

[32] See, e.g., Urbaser S.A. and Consorcio de Aguas Bilbao Bizkaia, Bilbao Biskaia Ur Partzuergoa v. The Argentine Republic, ICSID Case No. ARB/07/26, ¶ 1189 (Dec. 8, 2016) (The Urbaser tribunal found: "As far as recourse to the 'general principles of international law' is concerned, such reference would be meaningless if the position would be retained that the BIT is to be construed as an isolated set of rules of international law for the sole purpose of protecting investments through rights exclusively granted to investors").

[33] See e.g., DGM GLOBAL, http://www.dgmglobal.org (stating that among other mechanisms, the World Bank supports Indigenous peoples through a Dedicated Grant Mechanism (DGM) for Indigenous Peoples).

[34] Victoria Tauli-Corpuz (Special Rapporteur of the Human Rights Council), *Report of the Special Rapporteur on the Rights of Indigenous Peoples – International Investment Agreements, Including Bilateral Investment Treaties and Investment Chapters of Free Trade Agreements*, ¶¶ 65, U.N. Doc. A/HRC/33/42 (Aug. 11, 2016). (discussing the problems associated with international economic law).

rights law. Deep engagement with the institutions and frameworks that anchor globalization should be an avenue, a primary highway for the international indigenous rights movement to continue its engagement with international law as a tool for transformational change. As I explain in the next section, this involvement may require different strategies depending on the structure, mode and operation of the particular regimes.

5.2 TRANSFORMATIVE IMPACTS

For Indigenous peoples, the institutionalization of their interests within international economic law has yielded mixed results. Positive results include the incorporation of legal protections into legal frameworks, both in the drafting of newer frameworks and in the interpretation of older ones. For example, international IP has incorporated norms that encourage fair distribution of collective benefits, and international finance has made safeguards that encourage autochthonous decision-making routine. Trade panels – and to some extent investment tribunals – now recognize that the protection of indigenous interests is a legitimate ground to regulate and differentiate between products, services and investments (and the lawful practices associated with them) or that carve-out policies in favor of Indigenous peoples that may be characterized by competing interests as treaty violations are nevertheless permissible.

Negative results include the limited success in translating certain terms aimed at resisting economic and political impacts (e.g., collective property, traditional production practices, self-determination, consultation, etc.) into more effective provisions within each of the regimes. That indigenous "terms of resistance" have not been directly accommodated reflects, in part, the mistaken view that distributional concerns are irrelevant (or, at the very least, an afterthought) to international economic law; that these are matters to be addressed by domestic social policy. This oversight directly affects the making, the structure and ultimately the effectiveness of international economic law as it becomes generally disengaged from addressing its negative consequences. It has led to limited direct participation of indigenous groups in treaty-making and dispute settlement processes, resulting in imperfect solutions, all of which only narrowly address indigenous demands.[35]

---

[35] Lillian Aponte Miranda, *Indigenous Peoples As International Lawmakers*, 32 U. PA. J. INT'L L. 203, 260 (2010). For a conceptual analysis of the difference between forms of exceptions, see Caroline Henckels, *Should Investment Treaties Contain Public Policy Exceptions?* 59 B.C. L. REV. 2825 (2018).

Despite this mixed assessment for Indigenous peoples, I conclude this Chapter explaining in more detail the particular ways in which Indigenous peoples have contributed to transform – in my view, positively – international economic law and its institutions. To that effect, I use three particular perspectives proposed by Antony Taubman in his eloquent study of the effects of Indigenous peoples on the debates on international IP.

5.2.1 *New Standards, Metrics and Tools*

While limited, the direct and indirect (via interpretations) incorporations of legal protections into international economic frameworks has had an impact in different dimensions of the field of international economic law. For example, the incorporation of indigenous interests in international IP has resulted in new types of patents that show how poor countries are "exercising their interests in their heritage of genetic resources and traditional knowledge systems."[36] It also pushes against an expansive view of individual protection embedded in some Western legal systems of property rights. By incorporating norms like fair distribution, collective benefits as well as the protection of forms of collective property, international economic law has also expanded the debates about the stakeholders of international economic frameworks and the fairness of their impacts.

Allow me to unpack this broad generalization.

The significance of the recognition of concepts such as collective benefits, consultation and peoples, among other relevant concepts outside the mainstream vocabulary of (until now) contemporary practice of international economic law are modest of course, but not insignificant. They push against international economic law as a "procedural functionalist enterprise"; one predominantly concerned with individual rights, with private property and formal reciprocity.[37] In the words of Taubman, they defy the "atomistic" view of international economic law "concerned solely with private rights for individuals and commercial firms, and essentially necessarily lacking a collective or communal character."[38]

---

[36] See Anthony Taubman, 'New Dialogues, New Pathways: Reframing the Debate on Intellectual Property and Traditional Knowledge' *Washburn Law Journal*, Vol. 58 (2019) 373–97. For instance, the Agreement between Japan and Thailand that specifically establishes a Sub-Committee on Intellectual Property for the purposes of the effective implementation and operation of matters related to traditional knowledge, genetic resources and folklore. See Agreement between Japan and the Kingdom of Thailand for an Economic Partnership, art. 143, https://www.mofa.go.jp/region/asia-paci/thailand/epa0704/agreement.pdf.

[37] Bruce L. Benson, The Enterprise of Law: Justice without the State 21 (1990).

[38] Taubman *supra* note 36.

This limited transformation provides avenues to think differently about global economic interdependence (in less mercantilist ways) and its stakeholders (in broadly defined ways), and to assess the impacts of economic frameworks with new standards beyond traditional metrics – market efficiency, investment volumes, economic growth. By introducing new concepts relevant to the impacts of globalization on less obvious constituencies, more precise economic ideas that take seriously distributional considerations have been moderately embraced.

Distinct in its nature (vis-à-vis economic, labor or other organizations), the participation of Indigenous peoples has granted a face that humanizes the distributional impacts of economic frameworks. Since these effects permeate across regions, international economic law is forced to acknowledge the growing concentration of wealth; the hidden externalities (e.g., climate change); the lack of competitive condition in many important markets; the stagnation of income for some and inability to participate in modern markets for others; and the changing patterns in social mobility – just to mention a few. These are all now well accepted problems identified among mainstream economists, that remained unconnected to the field of international economic law, in part because of the dogmatic simplification of economic thinking and in part because of the social, political and institutional dynamics that result from economic treaties.

This opening has the potential to result in a virtuous spiral if taken seriously as more empirical evidence on the effects of the main frameworks of globalization becomes available. Suresh Naidu, Dani Rodrik, and Gabriel Zucman explain that this is the case:

> [b]ecause systematic empirical evidence is a disciplining device against ideological policy prescriptions embedded in preconceived theorizing. The empirical bent of economics makes it more difficult to ignore inconvenient facts, when real world markets do not behave like textbook ones. It is harder to idolize markets when research finds international trade produces large adverse effects on some local communities, minimum wages do not reduce employment, or financial liberalization produces crises rather than faster economic growth – just to point out a few empirical findings from the recent economic literature.[39]

Less noticeable but perhaps equally important is that these new tools within international economic law enable a better contextualization of the relevant

---

[39] Suresh Naidu et al., *Economics for Inclusive Prosperity: An Introduction*, Research Brief (Jan. 2019).

relationships between domestic law and indigenous communities. In particular, some of the changes motivated by the activism of Indigenous people tend to recognize the need for protection against illegitimate or unfair appropriation of resources via institutionalized action enabled or, at the very least, tolerated by states. This duty, which, it may be said, is borrowed from human rights law, pushes against the narrow view of international economic law that reinforces notions of false reciprocity of transactions between unequal parties, limited views of sources of legal obligations and the misconception of sovereignty of the state without due regard to people's self-determination embedded in many frameworks. This change can facilitate conversations for: (1) according due respect and recognition for true ownership of resources (think of traditional knowledge); (2) precluding unjust or uneven enrichment and illegitimate entitlements (think of consultations); and (3) recognizing notions of systemic equity and balance (think of sharing of benefits or policy carve-outs).[40]

What I find most interesting is that these changes have not had to transform the idea that the primary value embedded in international economic frameworks is freedom. Yet, Indigenous peoples' struggles help to contextualize our modern world, which is filled with power and capability imbalances, as directly connected to colonial practices and discrimination, which left a footprint in the formal institutions of today. Obviously, this process is not new but by creating more formal recognition by internationally backed legal categories it has been used to legitimize injustice – but by creating more formal categories or processes to directly or rhetorically challenge globalization, newer tools are incorporated into the shelf of international economic law to resist exploitation.

Finally, as Indigenous people have demanded recognition of autochthonous decision-making and participation in international economic law issues, the notion of stakeholders of the field (and perhaps also of economic globalization) has broadened. As I explain shortly, this has transformed the practice of international economic lawmaking in multiple, albeit limited ways. However, it has also created new avenues to avoid clashes between governments and Indigenous peoples and with that avoid violence. This of course has to be measured against the larger effects created by the cycle of susceptibility and exclusion, but to the extent that indigenous rights advocates start seeing institutions like the WB's Inspection Panel and GRS or the WTO as potentially useful to advance their interests, there is an intrinsic process that

---

[40] Taubman *supra* note 36.

legitimizes these institutions and international economic law more generally. As this process of legitimization is dialectic, this also helps to reinforce the concept that Indigenous peoples are important, rightful stakeholders of the system. Like environmental or labor advocates who have expanded the focus of international economic institutions in different but related ways, Indigenous peoples have brought the idea that marginalized communities must be part of the debate and their rights are potentially at stake with poorly regulated interconnected markets. What is remarkable about this, is that Indigenous peoples have been able to do so in ways that no other vulnerable communities – women, people with disabilities and national and ethnic minorities, etc. – have done. This allows for the exchange of new ideas and the sharing of experiences among communities at the margins of globalization.

5.2.2 *The Practice of International Economic Lawmaking*

The involvement of Indigenous peoples in both the formal and informal processes in international economic law has reshaped the practice of law-making in different ways. Yet, the engagement with the different regimes (trade, investment, IP and finance) has not been uniform in strategy and mode, nor in intensity and effectiveness across the distinct fields. This is in part due to the differences in operation and structure of each of the regimes. Before analyzing the impacts of indigenous rights advocacy on the practice of international economic lawmaking more generally, a reflection about different possibilities and limits imposed on indigenous advocates by such architectural aspects is in order.

As I have argued elsewhere,[41] international trade and investment regimes address indigenous concerns by creating exceptions, enabling decisions that conflict with the regimes' economic goals. Notably, trade and investment utilize this strategy within "stronger" or more legalized systems of enforcement (though often weighted in favor of corporate or state interests) – what I have called a "substantive, state-driven" or, in the words of Professor Paul Stephan, a "downstream" solution.[42] This contrasts somehow dramatically with the mechanisms within finance and IP, where indigenous concerns have been institutionalized by expanding participation and recognizing mechanisms for direct benefits of productive activities (though often ineffective or

---

[41] Sergio Puig, *International Indigenous Economic Law*, 52 U.C. DAVIS. L. REV. 1243, 1255 (2019).
[42] Paul B. Stephan, *Privatizing International Law*, 97 VA. L. REV. 1573, 1586 (2011).

circumventable) – a "procedural, market-driven" or, again in the words of Stephan, an "upstream" solution. Concretely, international IP and finance institutionalize indigenous interests utilizing a few concrete standards and procedures, within "weaker" or less legalized systems of enforcement.

The question of structure is not disconnected with that of the effectiveness of the regimes and strategy of its users. The "upstream" or "procedural, market-driven" approach tends to be better to address the direct effects of the proposed framework for understanding the process of marginalization by exclusion; namely, political illegitimacy and economic discrimination.[43] For instance, rules within finance require the involvement of indigenous communities in rule- and decision-making of IFIs, which helps legitimize the work of these international organizations, but also redirects necessary resources to indigenous communities in need.[44] IP rules protect indigenous culture and empower tribes in negotiations over IP protections, which reduce unfair appropriation but also can generate sources of income if these mechanisms are used effectively.[45] These examples are more "market-driven" in the sense that they require continuous engagement in different processes, including the process that results in what international lawyers often refer to as "soft law" (the development of guidelines, safeguards, best practices, standards and customary norms).

The capacities necessary to effect these institutions and their processes are also different. The "procedural, market-driven" approach requires the promotion of stakeholder engagement, consultation with traditional authorities and negotiated outcomes between non-state actors.[46] International IP and international finance rules have the potential to enhance fairness and promote efficiency if (and only if) existing imbalances in access to information, resources, influence and capabilities are calibrated – suggesting the need for the development of particular advocacy competences. Because these rules are notably difficult to enforce, and easy to evade, dominant actors apparently disfavored by rules can avoid them by regime "shifting" or "shopping" – from WIPO to TRIPS, from IFIs to capital markets.[47] The enforcement of rules is also transaction-costly, pointing to the need of the development of the following capabilities: independent technical expertise, skilled

---

[43] See *supra* Chapter 2.
[44] See *supra* Chapter 3.
[45] See *supra* Chapter 4.
[46] See NEIL K. KOMESAR, IMPERFECT ALTERNATIVES: CHOOSING INSTITUTIONS IN LAW, ECONOMICS, AND PUBLIC POLICY 98 (1994).
[47] Laurence R. Helfer, *Regime Shifting: The TRIPS Agreement and New Dynamics of International Intellectual Property Lawmaking*, 29 YALE J. INT'L L. 1, 6 (2004).

experience in negotiating business transactions and developed standardized procedures for community empowerment, decision-making and monitoring – just to name a few.

The "substantive, state-driven" or "downstream" solution is different along these dimensions. Trade and investment regimes are able to limit governmental actions and guard against possible abuse in the use of exceptions, but are less able to actively enforce mandates to support specific groups such as Indigenous peoples. This approach struggles to define the limits of state intervention in markets and economic life in affirmative terms. One probable consequence of this difficulty is that addressing the indirect yet concrete negative effects of globalization – reregulation and economic inequality – through lessening market-driven inequalities in income, wealth and access to goods and services like health care and education, is left mostly to domestic policy, not international agreements *per se*.[48] While not always undesirable this approach imposes additional challenges and hardships for, and demands different capabilities from, indigenous advocates. Indigenous peoples must sustain an active role in setting international norms, safeguarding regulatory autonomy and crucially, maintaining constant representation before domestic authorities (as opposed to international organizations). In addition, with the judicialization of these two fields embedded in systems with more legalized enforcement systems, participation in dispute settlement procedures, as well as the initiation of strategic litigation to test the limits of legal obligations, promotes a sensible relationship between treaties, and positively expands the flexibilities included in treaties, is much more relevant.[49] Access to legal and policymaking expertise is therefore critical in those regimes that incorporate indigenous interests in a downstream fashion.[50]

To be sure, protecting indigenous interests is a key litmus test for the very legitimacy of international economic law. As put more eloquently by Professor Bethany Berger, the alternative is regimes concerned solely with facilitating

---

[48] Karen Alter, *The European Union's Legal System and Domestic Policy: Spillover or Backlash?* 54 INT'L ORG. 489, 494–95 (2000). For a similar argument outside of international economic law, see Michael Howlett & Jeremy Rayner, *Globalization and Governance Capacity: Explaining Divergence in National Forest Programs as Instances of "Next-Generation" Regulation in Canada and Europe*, 19 GOVERNANCE 251, 252–53 (2006).

[49] On trade judicialization, see generally, Gregory Shaffer, *What's New in EU Trade Dispute Settlement? Judicialization, Public – Private Networks and the WTO Legal Order*, 13 J. EUR. PUBLIC POL'Y 67(2006). For a similar argument, see Robert Howse, *Human Rights, International Economic Law and Constitutional Justice: A Reply*, 19 EUR. J. INT'L L. 945, 952–53 (2008).

[50] Errol E. Meidinger, *Accord: Look Who's Making the Rules: International Environmental Standard Setting by Non-governmental Organizations*, 4 HUMAN ECOLOGY REV. 52 (1997).

transactions rather than with just distribution to indigenous and other marginalized groups.[51] Accepting a focus on transactional efficiency to the exclusion of distribution also fuels the fear that globalization is only about wealth transfers to elites as opposed to a mechanism to enhance liberty and opportunity. This in turn, encourages the embrace of isolationism seen in movements from the right and the left. Yet, the case of Indigenous peoples shows that international economic bodies can incorporate human rights norms, enforce them against non-state actors and catalyze private and state adoption of those norms. Even if imperfect, they present a case for looking beyond human rights documents to enforce international human rights norms.[52]

Indigenous peoples have helped to recalibrate international economic law through a recursive process based on concepts outside of the mainstream of international economic law, but within general international law. This process has the potential to permanently expand the focus of international economic law to include distributional concerns, distinct from other organized groups such as labor or environmental justice. For example, by effecting lawmaking in WIPO though the Intergovernmental Committee on Intellectual Property and other mechanisms, indigenous advocates influenced the development of norms on traditional knowledge. Not only did this effort give impetus to multiple domestic law changes, but also to the recognition of indigenous IP rights in the United Nations Declaration on the Rights of Indigenous peoples. At the WTO, the Extension of the Protection of Geographical Indications has moved the debates regarding the need to accommodate different regimes and recognize that the TRIPS Agreement interconnected with other treaties including the Convention on Biological Diversity. By necessary implication, this has expanded the debate over the protections offered to genetic resources as manifested in the multiple proposals part of the WTO's Doha Work Programme concerning development. Finally, at the WB, indigenous advocates have been active in the "bottom-up" design of safeguards and with that transforming the culture of development organization – acknowledging that a top-down support is also essential for bottom-up participatory projects to be effectively implemented at scale. These are just some examples – but are important as they reflect the transformation of the practice of lawmaking through the linkage of concepts and the broadening of the idea of stakeholders of this business and economic regimes.

---

[51] Bethany Berger, *Indigenous Harms from Global Development – Can International Economic Law provide Cure?* JOTWELL (July 24, 2019).
[52] *Id.*

5.2.3 *Social and Development Policy*

The involvement of Indigenous peoples in the processes of international economic law creation has, in turn, impacted upon international social and development policy in several ways. First, and most importantly, it has both educated and sensitized international economic law scholars, bureaucracies, advocates and other members of the epistemic communities – often insular, desensitized and elitist – of the liabilities imposed by the global economic activity on vulnerable groups as well as the resulting responsibilities toward the marginalized. In multiple ways, but ways that are distinct to labor or environmental interests, indigenous groups and their advocates have brought a unique perspective, providing a human face to those disenfranchised by the systemic "externalities" of globalization – poverty and inequality, loss of lands and forests, cultural appropriation – to the processes of bargaining over the future of trade, FDI and IP rules. This iterative process has led to a gradual demand for the participation of indigenous groups in international economic negotiations and the eventual normalization of their requests – sometimes in more successful ways than others – as necessary for the legitimacy of international institutions.

Relatedly, but certainly less effectively, these iterative processes have resulted in the recognition of Indigenous peoples – an example of marginalized, yet protected subjects of international law – as stakeholders of the system and as economic participants of globalization. The recognition, which goes far beyond past approaches that treated Indigenous peoples as objects, uninterested in economic participation, invited the necessary questions of what accommodations are necessary for indigenous communities that choose to develop wider commercial relationships. The result has been the contextual incorporation of provisions (mostly exceptions) that enable governments to make decisions to help overcome structural limitation. This is of course a work in progress, but one in which international economic law can transform domestic social and developmental policies that focus on economic empowerment of marginalized groups.

Such social and development dimensions are more apparent in the negotiations and policy debates in the traditional knowledge and geographic indication spheres, but it is becoming part of the general conversations in trade – in goods and finance (as IP provisions have made it into more general trade frameworks). For instance, in IP these debates include the need for protection of distinctive signs and traditional names as important entry points into the international trading system. In the words of Taubman:

It is striking that the two clusters of issues regarding the TRIPS Agreement that were framed in 2001 under the aegis of the Doha work programme—TRIPS and the CBD, and geographical indications—both have significance for traditional knowledge systems. The TRIPS-CBD debate specifically pivots on the question of what recognition, if any, the patent system might be required to give to the circumstances of access to, and use of, traditional knowledge and genetic resources. And, geographical indications have been explored as one tool for ensuring recognition in international markets of the distinctive qualities of Indigenous products when traded with the consent and involvement of communities.[53]

The recognition of indigenous protections in global IP frameworks has challenged the traditional understanding of the system. In fact, a more pluralistic understanding of what IP is for and whose interests it protects has inspired a similar conversation about commercial frameworks in general. Although it was ultimately not a hugely successful story, the special chapter on Indigenous peoples proposed by Canada during the USMCA negotiations provided an opening for future incorporation in such agreements.[54] It is not that a chapter of this nature in relevant agreements will necessarily increase the rights of Indigenous peoples already compatible with the system – although this might be the case – but will send a powerful message of the need to create regimes for populations at risk of the systemic effects of such a framework. It will also help with the incorporation of values and norms that are not typically associated with these agreements – such as customary law of indigenous and local communities and with that embedding the deeper values, spirituality and traditions of the indigenous system.

Here it is also relevant to signal the insistence of the Inter-American Commission of Human Rights (IACHR) that the duty of states to consult Indigenous peoples is applicable on free trade agreements when they affect their territories and natural resources. This position came in the context of the assessment of human rights as a result of the CP-TPP and it serves as a useful reminder that the norms are changing in this context.

Finally, the eventual incorporation of indigenous rights chapters in newer commercial frameworks (a conversation now on the table) could be used to force decisive actions on the part of governments to actualize their rights. For instance, more than twenty-five years ago labor chapters started transforming

---

[53] Taubman, *supra* note 36 at 394.

[54] Borrows, J. *Indigenous Diversities in International Investment and Trade*, in J. Borrows & R. Schwartz (eds.), Indigenous Peoples and International Trade: Building Equitable and Inclusive International Trade and Investment Agreements, 11–42 (2020).

trade agreements in incremental ways. Although that evolution was certainly slow, today some treaties like the USMCA contain relatively strong enforceable provisions with dedicated dispute settlement processes. This innovation of the USMCA was, in part, the result of pressures inflicted by the United States on Mexico to enhance labor rights in exchange for the benefit of market access (and as a result, the possible benefit of labor interest in the United States too). Similarly, future trade benefits can be conditioned on the enactment of provisions to effectuate meaningful domestic law change as well as to incorporate mechanisms to enforce indigenous rights when their violation has a trade relation. Thinking forward, indigenous advocates can rely on prior successes to transform social and development policy and leverage international economic arrangements and their dispute settlement provisions to that effect.

6

Indigenous Interests and the Future of Economic Treaties

The intersection between indigenous rights and international economic agreements is paradigmatic of the ways in which globalization accommodates issues of social and economic justice. This intersection provides insight into the fate of the marginalized communities in a system that privileges certain values and goals often incompatible with some indigenous values and goals – a topic to which I shall return in the final chapter of this book. What the prior chapters make evident, however, is that to address social and economic justice, international economic agreements can start by addressing indigenous interests in a systemic and more encompassing way and lead the way to frameworks for better social and economic inclusion. This is the key litmus test for the very legitimacy of international economic law after the crisis of the system that results from the growing anti-globalization sentiment.

I make some basic recommendations based on the prior analysis. These recommendations are only partial; insufficient to address the current wave of discontent with globalization's negative effects or the deep existing structural inequities between and within countries – especially as the global pandemic resulting from Covid-19 exacerbates them. I believe it would be disingenuous to issue a set of optimistic proposals given that the same dominant actors, who vastly benefit from the current uneven system of global interdependence, should also supply benevolent-spirited solutions that may go against their best short-term economic interests. It would be inconsistent and overly hopeful to believe that the motivations of actors within the modern economic system entail the surrendering of massive amounts of wealth and power. As Alberto Alesina puts it "The benevolent social planner does not exist."[1] But, within the realm of limited possibilities, there is incremental change, and I deeply

---

[1] Alberto Alesina & Enrico Spolaore, The Size of Nations (2003) at 31.

believe that the relative success of Indigenous peoples shows precisely that over time, change can happen. They teach the importance of "resistance from *within*" – this is, the use of concepts enshrined in human rights discourse, norms, legal rules and norms, and strategies to address the failures of economic interdependence.

6.1 THE SYNTHESIS OF MARGINALIZATION

The intersection between international economic law and indigenous rights points out the overarching vision that still permeates across international economic law: a vision of hermetically sealed regimes.[2] This silo approach impedes the observation that, though international economic law may be efficient in a practical, yet limited way (Kaldor-Hicks),[3] it nonetheless transfers relative influence and power from the disenfranchised and underrepresented – organized labor, areas with modest or poor infrastructure – to the empowered actors that benefit from interconnected markets – MNCs, financiers, economic capitals.[4] Moreover, this compartmentalized and oft-overspecialized understanding of the field promotes a vision of economic interdependence that is reciprocal and consensual and that lacks relationships with and links to other fields of international law – from indigenous rights to health regulation, from anticorruption to tax evasion. This vision is reflected in many international economic arrangements, which generally fail directly to address human-focused areas of international law.[5]

A narrow, specialized and hermetic version of international economic law facilitates complex negotiations, but its result, ignored by some strands of legal scholarship,[6] is the weakening of the tools available within international law to protest against the unequal distribution of resources and the consequent marginalization and inequality. It is not value neutral; instead, it allocates

---

[2] See Giorgio Sacerdoti, *WTO Law and the "Fragmentation" of International Law: Specificity, Integration, Conflicts*, in WTO: GOVERNANCE, DISPUTE SETTLEMENT & DEVELOPING COUNTRIES 595, 596 (Merit E. Janow, Victoria Donaldson & Alan Yanovich eds., 2008).

[3] See generally J. R. Hicks, *The Foundations of Welfare Economics*, 49 ECON. J. 696, 700 (1939). For the trade application, see Alan O. Sykes, *Comparative Advantage and the Normative Economics of International Trade Policy*, 1 J. INT'L ECON. L. 49, 57–64 (1998).

[4] See Gregory Shaffer, *How the WTO Shapes Regulatory Governance*, 9 Reg. & Governance 1, 3 (2015) at 16.

[5] For a discussion in the context of international trade law, see Harold Hongju Koh, *Global Tobacco Control as a Health and Human Rights Imperative*, 57 HARV. INT'L L.J. 433, 440–41 (2016) at 437–38.

[6] See, e.g., Robert O. Keohane, *Reciprocity in International Relations*, 40 INT'L ORG. 1 (1986) (providing a narrow discussion of international law).

responsibility to address the political economy (and resulting transfers of influence and power) created by international economic law to domestic social policy, and enables international economic agreements to refrain from prescribing certain types of policies. As Purdy et al. put this point, which is not unique to international economic agreements, many modern neoliberal institutions that appeal to efficiency:

> promise to avoid controversial political and ethical judgments. In the case of Kaldor-Hicks, they do so by relying on criteria that theoretically could make everyone better off. The implicit vision is of a neutral constitutional order encasing a market system that enables the realization of many different conceptions of the good in a liberal-pluralist frame. The affirmative idea that a market order secures an important form of the liberal value of neutrality interacts here with the negative idea that any political judgments about which social interests to secure or advance are likely to involve capture, entrenchment, and spurious claims to a (probably non-existent) "public interest," ... As we have argued above and elsewhere, this version of neutrality conceals and enforces significant judgments about who gets what (distribution) and who gets to do what to whom (coercion).[7]

The limited inclusion of Indigenous peoples' interests (or, for that matter, of other vulnerable populations) from international economic instruments is defensible only to a point. The underlying assumption is that domestic law and/or other international instruments will address the imbalances created by globalization adequately, which is concerned with efficiency, that is, wealth maximization. Such maximization "may have seemed a plausibly desirable goal of economic policy because, in fact, new income seemed to be widely shared ... [and] redistributing through the tax code to compensate losers, while of course never approaching its Paretian utopia, was a plausible rough description of how the redistributive state might operate."[8] However, in a fragmented context, where this redistribution is rarely the case, the exclusion of systemic treatment of indigenous interests from economic arrangements looks less like a matter of simplification or epistemic quality and, for some, more like strategic design – a system created by the "globalized elites" to exploit the vulnerable.

---

[7] Jedediah Britton-Purdy, David Singh Grewal, Amy Kapczynski & K. Sabeel Rahman, *Building a Law-and-Political-Economy Framework: Beyond the Twentieth-Century Synthesis*, 129 Yale L.J. 1784, 1813 (2020) (stating that in a democratic political economy, "the political community must be able to assert its collective will over the economic order" and "the substance of economic life must support democratic self-rule").

[8] *Id.*

In this context, the intense focus on efficiency and wealth maximization of international economic arrangements begins to suggest that upwards redistribution of utility is in fact the goal rather than an unfortunate byproduct. It is not surprising, therefore, that groups claiming communities affected by globalization are joining forces with nationalist currents that reject "globalism," promote slogans such as "buy American, hire American," and defend a renewed version of economic protectionism with a xenophobic undertone.[9] Correctly or not, these groups see in interdependence a massive economic transfer – from wealthy (United States) to emerging powers (China); from Athens to Brussels; from the poor (99 percent) to the rich (1 percent) – but none see in its current architecture a plausible avenue to resist the imbalances exacerbated by it. Hence, both suggest that nations should "protect ... against supposedly vicious competition from others," instead of investing in a better functioning and fairer international economic order.[10]

But it is hard for me to see how that rhetoric against international law will actually change anything. Instead, Indigenous peoples in their long continuous struggle against systemic oppression teach the importance of "resistance from *within*" – the importation of building and deploying a particular language enshrined in human rights discourse, norms, legal concepts and strategies into the frameworks of economic interdependence.[11] Despite this clear lesson, it is especially alarming that in debating globalization's future, scholars and policymakers have not only protested against treaty frameworks that support globalization (e.g., NAFTA, EU, CP-TPP), but also against human rights law and enforcement, citing potential "costs to the friendly relations of states and even interstate peace."[12] In effect, both camps are in partial agreement that international law is the problem – a viewpoint that poses a challenge to interstate cooperation not seen in recent history.

This viewpoint is of limited purchase. This position ignores the important links of international economic law with human rights values as a mechanism to equalizing the vast disparities in material resources between and within

---

[9] Exec. Order No. 13,788, 82 Fed. Reg. 18,837 (Apr. 18, 2017).

[10] Robert Howse, *Senate Democrats Prepare a Trade War beyond Trump's Wildest Fantasies*, Int'l Econ. L. & Pol'y Blog (2017), http://worldtradelaw.typepad.com/ielpblog/2017/08/-senate-democrats-prepare-a-trade-war-beyond-trumps-wildest-fantasies-.html.

[11] See Maria Camila Bustos, U.N. Climate Negotiations: Indigenous Resistance from Within, NACLA (Jan. 11, 2014), https://nacla.org/news/2014/1/11/un-climate-negotiations-indigenous-resistance-within.

[12] Ingrid Wuerth, *International Law in the Post-Human Rights Era*, 96 Tex. L. Rev. 279, 279 (2017) (arguing that international law "should focus on a stronger, more limited core of international legal norms that protects international peace and security, not human rights").

countries – a goal indeed reflected in frameworks like the WTO Agreements.[13] The position effectively renounces the common values espoused and supported by international law. Briefly, three reasons reflected in this work should make the case against this retrenched position. All these reasons combined, suggest that an increased focus on human rights in international economic law is a preferable alternative to the dominant positions currently taken: the practically impossible and economically costly one that demands an immediate retrenchment of globalization, and the politically obsolete and unsustainable one that allocates responsibility to address the negative effects of globalization exclusively to domestic policy.[14]

First, this work has shown that, to some degree, human rights norms are enforceable in the frameworks of international economic law. The IP model illustrates the ability to actualize the principles and values of human rights law in the domestic enforcement of economic agreements. Moreover, not all models of law enforcement require interstate conflicts that can lead to diplomatic instability. For example, international finance influences corporate behavior with no need for interstate confrontations and their associated politicization.[15]

Second, the enforcement of human rights does not necessarily entail the expansion of existing legal obligations – there are sufficient recognized protections in different sources of legal authority that can be deployed more effectively. The effects of iterative engagement within international economic institutions can be leveraged without creating an enforcement process for each human rights commitment. International economic institutions like the WTO can delineate targets and policies for supporting human rights within their constitutive frameworks, including the policy that protecting human rights justifies the limiting or conditioning of rights or benefits under international economic arrangements to economic actors. In fields like investment, along with clearer indigenous rights

---

[13] The preamble reads: "[r]ecogniz[e] that their relations in the field of trade and economic endeavour should be conducted with a view to raising standards of living." See Panel Report, *Brazil – Certain Measures Concerning Taxation and Charges*, ¶ 7.568, WTO Docs. WT/DS472/R & WT/DS497/R (Aug. 30, 2017) [hereinafter *Brazil Taxation Panel Report*] ("The Panel therefore finds that Brazil has demonstrated that a concern exists in Brazilian society with respect to the need to bridge the digital divide and promote social inclusion, and that such concern is within the scope of 'public morals' as defined and applied by Brazil.").

[14] On retrenchment, see Richard Tuck, *The Left Case for Brexit*, DISSENT MAG., June 6, 2016, visit https://www.dissentmagazine.org/online_articles/left-case-brexit. On response, see, e.g., Sykes, *supra* note 3, at 67.

[15] See Galit A. Sarfaty, *The World Bank and the Internalization of Indigenous Rights Norms*, 114 Yale L.J. 1791, 1799 (2005) (citing Benedict Kingsbury, *Operational Policies of International Institutions as Part of the Law-Making Process: The World Bank and Indigenous Peoples, in* The Reality of International Law: Essays in Honour of Ian Brownlie (Guy S. Goodwin-Gill & Stefan Talmon eds., 1999)) at 1792.

exceptions an explicit "human rights jurisdictional veto" could be adopted. This veto would direct tribunals to summarily dismiss arbitral proceedings from investors implicated in violations of human rights.[16] BITs could also force MNC to consent to counterclaims for their human rights violations and governments can force these actors to adjudicate some alleged human rights violations under newly designed international systems.[17]

Third, the argument that human rights enforcement can impair peace and security fails to recognize that growing inequality itself is the principal factor that impairs peace and security.[18] Abdicating the enforcement of human rights overlooks the fact that such rights are a moral imperative, essential for peace and security and good for business (in that order). The international trade system has recognized the importance of human rights and has been adapted to accommodate indigenous interests. The reform of the investment arbitration system signals a similar accommodation.[19] These accommodations evidence how human rights battles are not only about the recognition of abstract values, but the defense of concrete forms of economic participation and subsistence.[20]

The case studies of Indigenous peoples reveal the systemic challenges posed by global economic interdependence, and the relative success Indigenous peoples have had in confronting those challenges. The specific nature of these challenges and successes derive from the distinct context of indigenous rights and their unique status and struggles. Yet, in understanding them, it is also possible to draw generalizable lessons for international economic law, and glean global strategies for improving the treatment of all marginalized groups, not just Indigenous peoples. What might globalization that takes marginalized groups seriously look like? What issues would it foreground, and how would it address them? In the next four sections I offer a possible set of broad

---

[16] The idea of a "veto" as a special jurisdictional issue is not new. For instance, under Article 1110 of NAFTA, a tax veto applies to fiscal measures in claims of improper expropriation. NAFTA does not suggest that tax matters cannot be arbitrated. Rather, the treaty says that fiscal authorities in host and investor states together may block the arbitral proceedings. See generally William W. Park, *Arbitration and the Fisc: NAFTA's "Tax Veto,"* 2 CHI. J. INT'L L. 231, 231–32 (2001).

[17] Center for International Legal Cooperation *The Hague Rules on Business and Human Rights Arbitration (December, 2019),* https://www.cilc.nl/project/the-hague-rules-on-business-and-human-rights-arbitration.

[18] See *UN Experts Urge More Action on Inequalities That Threaten Peace and Security, Development, and Human Rights,* UN-OHCHR, Dec. 2018, visit https://www.ohchr.org/EN/NewsEvents/Pages/DisplayNews.aspx?NewsID=23969&LangID=E.

[19] *Working Group III: Investor-State Dispute Settlement Reform,* UNCITRAL, May 2020, visit https://uncitral.un.org/en/working_groups/3/investor-state.

[20] See Paola Conconi & Tania Voon, *EC – Seal Products: The Tension between Public Morals and International Trade Agreements,* 15 WORLD TRADE REV. 211, 213 (2016).

reorientations. These suggestions are organized following the matrix designed to understand the effects of globalization in Chapter 2. It aims to inspire a dialogue between legal scholarship, international organizations, grassroots movements like the indigenous rights movement and other stakeholders of globalization like MNCs to construct a more equal globalization.

6.2 LEGITIMACY: TOWARD THE EMPOWERMENT OF THE MARGINALIZED

By centering efficiency as a core value, international economic law tends to marginalize questions of power, impacting its legitimacy. This is because questions of power are central to it and are connected to the inability of many to exit the cycle of susceptibility and exclusion.

International economic law can start by enhancing input as well as external legitimacy with rules that are more sensible to the challenges faced by marginalized groups. First, however, governing structures must, to the extent possible, include representatives of marginalized groups in the upstream and downstream law production processes – that is, in treaty negotiations and international dispute settlement proceedings. With some caveats, the participation of Indigenous peoples in the development of safeguards within financial organizations, enhanced with better procedural tools to bring complaints and arguments before enforcement and compliance mechanisms, serves as a model for this expansion.

This move could be transformative. While it is hard to sustain that in all contexts of international economic negotiations states have a duty to consult with Indigenous peoples (in many contexts it may well be the case), the model of consultation with Indigenous peoples can enhance participation of vulnerable populations by following basic elements derived from this customary rule of international law. The basic elements include: (a) prioritizing the safeguard role of participation; (b) contextualizing participation within the larger body of human rights standards (especially procedurally) to mitigate inequalities; (c) accepting how international law recognizes the exercise of sovereign power in the state; and (d) recognizing the distinct rights, interests, and responsibilities among the stakeholders of the process. I briefly address these contours, which I have dealt with in more detail with Professor Anaya in our exploration of the duty to consult with Indigenous peoples.[21]

---

[21] S. James Anaya & Sergio Puig, Mitigating State Sovereignty: The Duty to Consult with Indigenous Peoples, 67 U. Toronto L.J. 435, 439–46 (2017) (hereinafter Mitigating State Sovereignty).

6.2.1 *The Safeguard Role of Consultations*

In general, public consultations are one of several mechanisms used to achieve an appropriate balance between the rights and obligations of different stakeholders in plural societies. Consultations in relation to Indigenous peoples are distinct in that they safeguard against violations of human rights, including Indigenous peoples' specific rights that have been internationally affirmed. The protected rights include, in addition to the right of self-determination, rights to property, culture, religion, nondiscrimination in relation to lands, territories and natural resources, and the right of Indigenous peoples to set and pursue their own priorities for economic, social and cultural development.[22]

Notably, a practical import of the safeguard role of this norm is that states are obligated (when the duty to consult applies) to take an active role, protecting the best interests of Indigenous peoples at all times and not only during the process of consultation.[23] For their part, consistent with the increasingly accepted view, business enterprises, at least as a matter of sound policy, have an independent responsibility to respect human rights.[24] Yet, the safeguard role should not eclipse the role of consultation as a balancing mechanism. This implies that, in addition to its safeguard role, the duty to consult also plays a remedial function when rights are affected. In other words, consultations serve to avert limitation of Indigenous peoples' rights and to align terms to offset, or compensate for, any resulting limitations or potential violations suffered by the indigenous party.

6.2.2 *Minimum Procedural Standards to Achieve Protection*

The UNDRIP, together with other sources of authority, demand certain requirements of consultations in order to adequately achieve the protective role. By demanding a minimum standard of protection, the duty to consult not only imposes procedural requirements against arbitrariness but also attempts to ensure balanced substantive outcomes among unequal stakeholders. The minimum procedural requirements that have been articulated by a number of sources include:

> *Good faith*: Indigenous participation must be done in good faith, through culturally appropriate procedures, and with the objective of reaching agreement on just terms.

---

[22] G.A. Res. 61/295, annex, Declaration on the Rights of Indigenous Peoples (Sept. 13, 2007).
[23] Mitigating State Sovereignty, *supra* note 21 at 15.
[24] U.N. Human Rights Council, Guiding Principles on Business and Human Rights, U.N. Doc. HR/PUB/11/04, at Principle 12 (June 16, 2011).

Direct engagement: States need to engage directly with Indigenous peoples.
Mitigation of power imbalances: In order for consultation procedures to adequately fulfill their safeguard role, the power imbalances (technical, political, or economic) among the actors involved must be mitigated.
Transparency: Indigenous peoples should enjoy full access to the information gathered in impact assessments that are done by state agencies or business enterprises.
Timing: To ensure the protection of rights, consultations must start before the state authorizes, or an enterprise undertakes or commits to undertake, any activity related to the measure.
Representativeness: Indigenous peoples should be consulted through their own representative decision-making institutions.

6.2.3 *Self-Determination and Consent*

In keeping with the safeguard role of the duty to consult, consent by Indigenous peoples, as a general rule, is required whenever their substantive rights over lands and resources, their rights to culture and religion, their right to set their own development priorities or other internationally recognized rights will be materially and substantially affected by the measure promoted by the state. On the other hand, international law's deferential stance toward state sovereignty allows exceptions to the general rule of indigenous consent where rights are affected, in as much as states may impose limitations on the exercise of certain human rights without consent within the established doctrine of international law and in accordance with explicit provisions of international human rights treaties. For such limitations to be in compliance with international human rights law, as Professor Anaya has explained, "first, the right involved must be one subject to limitation by the State and, second, as indicated by the Declaration [on the Rights of Indigenous Peoples], the limitation must be necessary and proportional in relation to a valid State objective motivated by concern for the human rights of others."[25]

Even if a valid and legitimate public purpose can be established for the limitation of, for example, property or other rights related to indigenous territories, the limitation must be necessary and proportional to that purpose. Any decision to limit Indigenous peoples' rights must ensure that other applicable safeguards are also implemented, in particular, steps to minimize or offset the limitation on the rights through impact assessments, measures of

[25] *Id.* at 11, para 34.

harm mitigation, compensation and benefit sharing (as I explain below). And decisions to limit Indigenous peoples' rights should be subject to review by an impartial authority – for instance, an independent judicial body.

6.2.4 *Shared Responsibilities*

A human rights approach to enhance the input legitimacy should take account of the interests and responsibilities of principal stakeholders, including but not exclusively the business community, who have their own economic objectives. These key stakeholders should all have a common interest in ensuring normatively sound and practical outcomes in which their respective rights and interests are accommodated, and their responsibilities are discharged in a balanced way. This type of participation might also be a means of building trust between the business and indigenous parties that can lead to mutually beneficial outcomes that are conducive to the enjoyment of human rights, especially in the social and economic realm.

6.3 NEUTRALITY: IMPROVING INDIGENOUS-TAILORED DESIGN

Markets are only truly neutral if they take power into consideration. Ultimately neutrality has to account for systemic imbalances and "endowments that shape all voluntary bargains, the market power that legal structures enable, and the political power that may arise from differential endowments."[26] In other words, in the context of a history of economic and political subjugation special protections need to ensure truly neutral arrangements even if it means re-politicizing institutions. Broadly speaking, this could be done in two ways: by creating tailored exceptions in international arrangements and by forcing legal reform through them.

6.3.1 *Tailored Exceptions*

To address the effects of economic discrimination, international economic agreements must reduce the burden of seemingly neutral provisions (e.g., performance requirements and antidiscrimination prohibitions). This could be done by demanding in economic agreements measures against practices and policies that adversely affect vulnerable populations. The Maori policy "carve-out" in the CP-TPP serves as the beginning of a model. New Zealand

---

[26] See Jedediah Britton-Purdy, et al., *supra* note 7 at 1820.

has successfully negotiated a clause regarding the Maori in the CP-TPP through a Treaty of Waitangi exception where the obligations of the New Zealand government toward the Treaty of Waitangi take precedence over all others.[27] This unique carve-out allows the government to implement policies that benefit Maori exporters without being obliged to offer equivalent treatment to individuals or corporations from other CP-TPP countries. Such carve-outs could go further and include specific obligations of impact assessment of trade, investment and IP deals on marginalized groups, as well as impact mitigation, and mechanisms for monitoring outcomes.

This particular point about impact assessment is rather important. Social and economic assessments of economic agreements should be performed as part of the analysis of major economic agreements, but especially those impacting large sectors of indigenous populations. In this process, international economic agreements, such as FTAs or BITs should mandate measures to safeguard against, or to mitigate the impacts that could adversely affect the rights of Indigenous peoples in relation to their territories as a condition for certain trade or investment benefits. Provisions for impact prevention and mitigation should be based on rigorous methodologies developed with the participation of affected members.

6.3.2 *Locking in Domestic Legal Reform*

More controversial, but perhaps more transformative is the possibility of locking in domestic legal reform in treaties such as regional trade deals. These commitments to policy reforms can be aimed at empowering Indigenous peoples in multiple ways – by, for instance, ensuring political participation, recognizing specific rights or ensuring fair policies – within the constitutional or legal provisions of the state agreeing to such frameworks. By creating incentives to transform domestic policy and regulation via the promise of trade advantages (think of the Brazilian case in Chapter 4), states with market and consumer power can force others to protect existing rights. For instance, the EU that uses its trade policy as a main source of global influence could continue such efforts included in the EU-Mercosur FTA (perhaps unsuccessful for other reasons). Another example that can be emulated is the recent labor chapter of the USMCA treaty. The chapter's most significant feature is Mexico's commitment

---

[27] See Maria Panezi, *The Complex Landscape of Indigenous Procurement*, in INDIGENOUS PEOPLES AND INTERNATIONAL TRADE: BUILDING EQUITABLE AND INCLUSIVE INTERNATIONAL TRADE AND INVESTMENT, John Borrows & Risa Schwartz (eds.) (Cambridge: Cambridge University Press, 2020) 242.

to overhauling its domestic labor laws and institutions. Unlike the Brazilian case with Bolsonaro (a "president" in open war with Indigenous peoples), the commitment in the USMCA is consistent with the new government's policy but it will lock in this domestic labor reform, making it less susceptible to being rolled back by future administrations.

One final clarification is in order: how to effectively ensure truly neutral international economic bargaining is fertile ground for further scholarship as well as for human rights advocacy. In this context, the mitigating goals of international human rights law offer a vehicle to further expand our understanding of the role of international economic law. Not only does such a lens allow us to problematize fundamental questions among different stakeholders, but it is also conducive to a harmonious understanding of the specific rights of historically disadvantaged peoples within international law.

6.4 DEMOCRACY: DEMO-REGULATION FOR THE RISE OF EQUALITY

International law, but especially international economic law, should have a basic commitment to democracy. By that I do not mean a particular set of political procedures and institutions, but an economic ordering accountable to those who live in that order. Such accountability is the democratic will of the people, expressed in procedures that accord equal weight to all members, and understand the particular challenges suffered by those in situations of exclusion, marginalization, vulnerability and precarity.

What would it mean to reorient international economic law and institutions toward an explicit pursuit of democracy, with an emphasis on *demo-regulation* – the use of legislative and regulatory practices in pursuit of equality – to overcome the contemporary crises? This question is really difficult to answer in general especially in two paragraphs. Nevertheless, the complexity of the problem should start by strengthening existing international institutions to understand the ways in which different societies determine their own priorities, while critically and creatively engaging with the way local communities engage with economic activity. While recognizing the virtues of well-functioning markets, these institutions should embrace the challenges of representativeness of international law. This does not mean that such institutions should be defined as inherently "progressive" or liberal, but instead should think of ways to engage with transformative politics, and social justice organizations on the ground. By doing so, international economic institutions can avoid falling into the trap that feeds the rejection of "globalism" by advocating for particular nationalism easily captured by protectionist interests.

In the meantime, to limit the use of international economic agreements to defend practices that exacerbate exploitation and disparity, governing structures as well as signatories must clarify the "policy-space" available to enact governmental measures that support vulnerable populations. Specifically, international economic rules should not interfere, nor be interpreted to interfere, with respect for basic human rights, social and economic rights in particular. Chapters in economic agreements that balance human rights with economic rules should make this clear; the model addressing measures necessary to protect indigenous rights under USMCA serves as a starting point. Admittedly, these efforts might be insufficient without a more active focus on domestic policies like tax, health care, access to education and infrastructure. Other actions could include flexibility within the use of tariffs to protect industries that employ indigenous groups affected by unfair competition.

Other efforts could include flexibility for a more active trade policy. As Rodrik explains, institutions like the WTO should adopt policies that target social dumping – a practice of employers using cheaper labor than is usually available at their site of production or sale.[28] This is not an easy role for international treaties as such policies must distinguish between true social dumping and regular market competition. However, trade remedies like anti-dumping and safeguards could be used to implement such policy goals with the aim of protecting marginalized communities. How that would work is a complex technical matter that I leave for another day. However, the broader point is that in many contexts, international economic arrangements should be more limited in economic ambitions and more ambitious in political goals, including flexibility to experiment with different models for empowerment.[29]

6.5 EQUALITY: SHARED BENEFITS AND BEYOND

Ultimately, international economic law must contribute to restructuring the imbalance of power that translates into the cycle of susceptibility and exclusion.

The measures outlined earlier should help to improve the situation. However, to reduce the impact of inequality, international economic arrangements could go further. Among other actions, mechanisms for improving bargaining power over the material resources of vulnerable or marginalized groups should be included via provisions that condition

[28] See generally DANI RODRIK, TOWARDS A MORE INCLUSIVE GLOBALIZATION: AN ANTI-SOCIAL DUMPING SCHEME (2018).
[29] *Id.*

economic benefits on the implementation of processes for fair compensation and direct sharing of benefits.

There is growing awareness that, in order for consultations to fulfill their safeguard role, any resulting indigenous consent should be in the form of an agreement with just terms premised on recognition of, and respect for, the implicated rights of Indigenous peoples.[30] The idea is to ensure full respect for Indigenous peoples' rights as well as to encourage genuine partnerships. Similarly, the inclusion in IP regimes of provisions of this nature for the benefit of indigenous groups serves as a preliminary exemplar of how fair compensation could be encouraged. States should complement this with mechanisms to enhance a symbiotic relationship between public and private actors and encourage joint management arrangements.

Such arrangements could be encouraged in concession agreements or as a condition to obtain certain rights. The rationale is simple: even if Indigenous peoples do not, under domestic law, own the resources to be extracted within their territories, as is the case of subsurface resources in most countries, they do provide access to the resources, and give up alternatives for the future development of their territories. Direct financial benefits – beyond incidental benefits like jobs or corporate charity – should accrue to Indigenous peoples because of the compensation due for adverse effects as well as for the significant social capital they contribute in the face of historical and contemporary circumstances.

Normatively, there is also a basis for this proposal. Indigenous peoples' rights of self-determination and self-governance mandate that they have a meaningful measure of authority and control over any activity within their territories or that otherwise affect the enjoyment of their rights. If state-permitted activities are to occur in this context, therefore, such activities should be carried out under joint management or similar arrangements in which Indigenous peoples have an ongoing say in how these activities are conducted. In this respect, there is a great deal of room for imagination and innovation in devising the terms of partnership in agreements.

Finally, in the context of partnership agreements, adequate grievance procedures, in accordance with the Guiding Principles on Business and Human Rights, should also be included in agreements within Indigenous

---

[30] See generally Inter-American Commission on Human Rights, *Indigenous and Tribal Peoples' Rights over Their Ancestral Lands and Natural Resources: Norms and Jurisprudence of the Inter-American Human Rights System*, IX. Right of Participation, Consultation and Consent, http://cidh.org/countryrep/Indigenous-Lands09/Chap.IX.htm.

peoples' territories.[31] In cases in which a private company is the operator, a company grievance procedure should be established to complement the remedies provided by the state. The grievance procedures should be devised and implemented with full respect for Indigenous peoples' own justice and dispute resolution systems.[32]

[31] *Guiding Principles on Business and Human Rights, supra* note 24 at para. 21.
[32] Mitigating State Sovereignty, *supra* note 21 at 26.

7

Toward an Indigenous-Based Critique of Globalization

The intersection between indigenous rights and international economic law serves as an instructive lens of the complex interactions between human and economic-focused areas of international law. Specifically, it uncovers how two fields with distinct goals, rules and structures are implicated in the way globalization both affects and tries to protect marginalized communities. Since both fields can also complement each other to improve the situation of almost one billion marginalized Indigenous people, international economic law can incorporate the struggle for social inclusion espoused by human rights law as it relates to Indigenous peoples. For that purpose, in Chapter 6, I provided a list of plausible innovations to lessen the negative impacts of globalization on this population and other disadvantaged groups.

At the same time, it is imperative that human rights advocates utilize legal instruments and institutions that promote economic interdependence to create or renew strategies that allow for the materialization of human rights. Not only must indigenous advocates engage with international law frameworks to advance their interests, but there is also relative success resulting from Indigenous peoples' participation in international economic lawmaking and its institutions that can be learned from. Importantly, such engagement with international economic law is necessary to develop, refine and magnify a distinct critique of globalization – a "resistance from *within*."[1] This critique is based on the recognition of both the positive and negative aspects of globalization. For one, markets have benefits but tend to have a dehumanizing character and to create a culture of "individual choice." International economic law has helped in creating benefits, but also maintains the racist

---

[1] See Maria Camila Bustos, U.N. Climate Negotiations: Indigenous Resistance from Within, NACLA (Jan. 11, 2014), https://nacla.org/news/2014/1/11/un-climate-negotiations-indigenous-resistance-within.

links of neoliberalism to colonialism. Finally, the critique accepts that there is a need to defend a role for international law, while recognizing the special challenges for its enforcement.

A resistance from within critique is based on human rights law, it should not be considered another discontent based on absolute losses – if anything, it is a critique based on *relative* losses.

In this final chapter, I briefly provide first, a reflection on how to rethink the failure of globalization with Indigenous peoples in mind. After that, I sketch the normative underpinnings of an inclusive globalization that can provide more hope for those marginalized by the current structure created by international economic law.

7.1 BEYOND THE CYCLE OF SUSCEPTIBILITY AND EXCLUSION

As discussed elsewhere in this work, international economic instruments themselves have paid attention to indigenous rights, often in surprisingly progressive ways. Despite this, it is remarkable how these fields handle Indigenous peoples as an afterthought. These economic treaties do not generally create or recognize existing rules or obligations on states or other powerful actors like MNCs that might alleviate the problems of the uneven distribution of resources, which is often exacerbated by current forms of globalization; at best, these instruments add exceptions to general rules. Such exceptions grant some extra (if limited) flexibility to experiment within domestic social policy to lessen the conditions of marginalization and in some contexts, allow states with capacity and strong domestic markets, to affect policy change abroad.

This general deficiency is structural and has a well-known intellectual history.[2] Primarily, it could be attributed to two ideas that permeate throughout international economic law – especially in the fields of international trade and investment law – and, with that, a limited vision of the role of international law in economic interdependence.

The first of these two ideas tends to oversimplify the goals of economic interdependence as a mechanism to unleash market forces and industrialization; it tends to reinforce a culture of "individual" choice (consumption based on internal benefit, but with limited concern for the external impact of the

---

[2] KIM PHILLIPS-FEIN, INVISIBLE HANDS: THE MAKING OF THE CONSERVATIVE MOVEMENT FROM THE NEW DEAL TO REAGAN (2009); THOMAS PIKETTY, CAPITAL IN THE TWENTY-FIRST CENTURY (Arthur Goldhammer trans., Harvard University Press 2014) (examining and documenting the rise in income inequality); David Singh Grewal & Jedediah Purdy, *Introduction: Law and Neoliberalism*, 77 LAW & CONTEMP. PROBS. 1, 2–3 (2014).

choice). This model has worked in some contexts, despite evidence that markets do not always mean more or better options; the devastating effects on our planet; or that industrialization can fail to increase general welfare. What is incorrect about this idea is that, having helped to create a massive transfer of power (economic and political) to actors that largely benefit from globalization, drafters of international treaties and policymakers can simply ignore the tools available to limit their effect or can stop innovating to improve the conditions on the ground, especially for traditional and agricultural (nonindustrial) communities.

The second idea involves a vision of hermetically sealed regimes, unconnected between them, unable to address problems derived from the lack of social inclusion. As already discussed, the mainstream understanding of international economic law often describes these instruments as reciprocal, efficient, neutral and fair, with limited relationships and links to other international law fields.[3] This vision may be dismissing the problems described in prior chapters as well as the multiple ways in which human-based areas of international law mandate specific policies, including policies to address marginalization with preventive and corrective actions.

One result of these two ideas is the belief that mechanisms that encourage redistribution are in essence domestic policy alternatives – not international law choices. But domestic policy is often part of the problem. This is because the current international economic frameworks reflect the domestic power imbalances, especially in wealthy countries that can dictate the terms of such treaties. Recently, the answer to this problem has been to reject globalization as opposed to improve the processes that lead to interdependency to achieve a fairer and more democratic world. This seems as suspect and shortsighted as the defense of globalization for its unprecedented ability to grow GDP, or to increase trade and investment volumes. It basically leaves politically disenfranchised groups to fight on their own on the domestic (national terrain) stage.

How is this disconnection relevant to the reality of Indigenous peoples? It is relevant because an indigenous critique of globalization should start by defending at minimum some value in international cooperation. In particular, international law and its legitimate institutions must be defended for their ability to broadcast injustice and appeal for compassion to a global audience as well as to mobilize actors and catalyze dynamics for domestic transformation. This is not to say that we can ignore or fail to acknowledge that international law has been, at points, part of the problem by normalizing injustice,

---

[3] See *Going Alone: The Case For Relaxed Reciprocity In Freeing Trade* (Jagdish Bhagwati ed., 2002).

reinforcing a consumption culture and exacerbating the structural racism and discrimination experienced by Indigenous peoples. However, as this work shows, international economic frameworks have the capacity to (and must) adapt and should become an important part of the solution to major challenges. For that to happen, international economic law needs to recognize that the structural inequality of the magnitude that we continue to experience cannot and should not be treated as normal. Both the nature and the scale of the problem are unique and demand transformative action.

Of course, international law cannot redress all wrongs. But it must try to address questions of systemic injustice and racism. Hence, calls for "downsizing" international law, including international economic law, fail to see the importance and moral value of a legal system that provides a check on power (states, MNCs and otherwise). Such reductionist views – expressed in some of the discontents summarized in Chapter 1 – undermine the deep function of international law to act as a mitigating force against the abuse of state sovereignty and dismiss the potential that international law has to transform ideas about justice and catalyze collective action around it. Downsizing the role of law in this context could mean the further retooling of international law into an adjunct of global business; an instrument of power under the disguise of suspect causes advanced by nationalists (think of protectionist discontent) or other more hawkish groups (think of geoeconomic discontent).

The second distinct aspect of this critique of globalization is that while Indigenous peoples have not been in general on the winning side of international economic law, they have made important contributions to its slow and imperfect transformation. This leads to two observations: first, international economic law shares values with international indigenous law and policy that can help to continue international economic law's evolution into a more capacious endeavor; one that rejects the orthodoxy that what is good for markets is good for progress. It is a convenient myth that progress magically springs up like flowers at the feet of commerce and must be rejected as a basic underpinning of international economic law. The second observation is its opposition to the structural pessimism and unchecked culture of individual choice that the popular or corporate power discontents expound, particularly as these critiques borrow from the long list of grievances of Indigenous peoples. The irony is that the groups using these grievances of disenfranchisement, dispossession and theft, use it to mobilize resources to further entrench the cause of moneyed interests.

In this sense, an indigenous critique must defend international law and must be cautiously optimistic about the capacity of this framework to adapt and transform societies. This indigenous critique, however, must also reject the idea that the sole alternative in a globalized economic system is the unchecked market. In the next section I provide some foundations for a different path.

7.2 INDIGENOUS PEOPLES AS CORE PARTICIPANTS OF GLOBALIZATION

The study of international indigenous economic law reveals the systemic challenges posed to Indigenous peoples by global economic interdependence, and the relative success Indigenous peoples have had in confronting those challenges. In understanding the limited success, it is also possible to draw generalizable lessons for international economic law, and glean global strategies for all marginalized groups, not just Indigenous peoples. We can also derive from this analysis some first principles – basic propositions that cannot be deduced from any other context – to help structure a healthier, more resilient globalization. In this different setting, Indigenous peoples, like many other actors, should be seen as aspiring to be core participants – not simply an afterthought.

The first necessary move is reject the idea that the cycle of marginalization is inevitable – such a cycle is the result of complex history as much as the conditions of key political, economic and social institutions, but it can be radically transformed. Because the shape and effects of globalization are not static and will change over time, international economic institutions should aspire to set as a core goal the development of free autonomous human beings. This requires rejecting the connection between markets and individual choice by tending to "the market" with flexibility. This more flexible view sees markets as one of many institutional choices to improve key human needs such as: education and health care, employment generation, credit facilitation, women's and indigenous empowerment. International economic agreements should assist in the goal of improving the distribution of the benefits of international interactions, which also depends on other policies, including policies for technological dissemination and human rights protections, as well as ecological and environmental protections.[4]

Thinking beyond the cycle of marginalization also requires tending to the gardens of democracy and participating in international lawmaking. Indigenous peoples, like other fellow men and women, should be given full voice to determine the way forward and with that obtain equal opportunity as

---

[4] THE MISERY OF INTERNATIONAL LAW: CONFRONTATIONS WITH INJUSTICE IN THE GLOBAL ECONOMY.

economic participants in globalization. Participation, engagement and experimentation can lead to the incorporation of more democratic values, for its ability to confront injustice exposes the boundaries of society and tolerance, the shortcomings of positions that stem from calls to our baser nature, and the virtues of policies that benefit the common good. In this sense, the commitment to legitimacy through democratization should be deeper than the commitment to commerce, markets and individual choice. As international economic law is inescapably political, the potential tensions should be resolved in favor of those democratic values, seeking always a reasoned search for truth. By the same token, indigenous advocates could continue to lobby developed countries, especially those that are home to Indigenous peoples, to facilitate the inclusion of protective treaty language, and to impose enforceable obligations on MNCs to respect such norms as a condition for benefits or rights.[5]

Finally, international economic law should enable the dissemination of core values of international law – human rights law in particular. International economic law and human rights have overlapping principles, including personal freedom and nondiscrimination; the belief that everyone matters and should have similar opportunities; and the value of diversity and tolerance in the sense that toleration must be reasonably offered (except when it leads to intolerance to others). Both policy and institutional changes are needed to recognize the need to actualize such common values. To varying extents, international economic law and institutions have already responded to the demand for such recognition. However, a blind spot of international economic law is the limited engagement with the different notions of responsibility toward the planet that Indigenous peoples often demonstrate. This correction would be necessary as we seek solutions to our current crises – from starvation, to massive irregular migrations; from inequality to structural racism; from climate injustice to global pandemics – while illuminating how Indigenous peoples can use their resources (economic, cultural and social) to bargain more effectively. At its root, such a process of transformation demands a deeper engagement with a core principle often found in Indigenous peoples communities. As I see it, their struggle for recognition and survival has led by necessity to a deep understanding of the individual's responsibility toward the community, to future generations and to the ecosystems that sustain and provide for both. This involves a radical rejection of selfishness and the

---

[5]   See generally Indian Law, *The Double Life of International Law: Indigenous Peoples and Extractive Industries*, 129 HARV. L. REV. 1755–78 (2016), https://harvardlawreview.org/wp-content/uploads/2016/04/1755-1778-Online.pdf.

modern culture of individual choice that often feeds the cycle of susceptibility and marginalization. Such notions of responsibility embrace a deeper connection with the communal as well as the intergenerational. Perhaps, the Covid-19 pandemic – which has forced us to confront our very own vulnerabilities as a species – can help to unleash that deeper engagement with such values and help us learn from Indigenous peoples.

Conclusion

International economic law is facing a critical juncture – a time of uncertainty that requires important decisions by states and international organizations that will have an impact on many for years to come. In addition to other challenges, the Covid-19 pandemic exacerbates the regressive effects of climate change that disproportionately impact the poor, whether in wealthy or emerging economies. Without adequate action to help the most vulnerable and marginalized segments of the population, including Indigenous peoples, the future of globalization looks rather bleak.

However, the current crises also offer an opportunity to remedy past failures and create new, more hopeful futures of globalization. This transformation is a key litmus test for the very legitimacy of international economic law itself. To succeed, policymakers will need to engage with legal frameworks addressing human and economic-focused areas of globalization – and the complex ways in which these fields interact with each other. Perhaps more importantly, policymakers will also need to employ new deontological viewpoints to issues more often addressed from traditional economic and limited cost-benefit analyses and perspectives.

What is imperative in reimaging the future of globalization in general, and the transformation of international economic law in particular, is the incorporation of indigenous perspectives including: (a) respect for distinct beliefs about and forms of economic organizations; (b) active commitment with communal self-determination; and (c) recognition of individual and corporate duties toward our planet and future generations. In my view, these are the three most powerful insights that international economic law has failed to understand by leaving Indigenous peoples at the margins of globalization.

Index

BOOKS IN THE SERIES

CPSIA information can be obtained
at www.ICGtesting.com
Printed in the USA
BVHW091826110522
636808BV00007B/101